Pamela's War

CHERRYL VINES

Pamela's War

A Moving Account of a Young Girl's Life in the Midlands During the Second World War

First published 2012

The History Press
The Mill, Brimscombe Port
Stroud, Gloucestershire, GL5 2QG
www.thehistorypress.co.uk

© Cherryl Vines, 2012

The right of Cherryl Vines to be identified as the Author
of this work has been asserted in accordance with the
Copyrights, Designs and Patents Act 1988.

British Library Cataloguing in Publication Data.
A catalogue record for this book is available from the British Library.

ISBN 978 0 7524 6813 6

Typesetting and origination by The History Press
Printed in Great Britain
Manufacturing managed by Jellyfish Print Solutions Ltd

Contents

Introduction

On her eighty-fifth birthday I take my Mother, Pamela Moore, for a drink at her old family home, The Woodman Hotel at Clent, now renamed The French Hen and stuffed with French antiques and bric-a-brac. She is not impressed.

She can clearly remember this building in its heyday in the 1930s, when it was in its prime. Freshly decorated and newly carpeted, full of customers drinking, smoking, laughing, living! Listening to dance music playing on the radiogram. I can almost feel their ghostly presence.

We leave by the back door and walk across the car park. 'This,' she says, 'is where I saw David for the last time.' David was the boy she loved and hoped to marry; this place is where they kissed for the first, and last, time. He is one of many young airmen who have laughed and joked and drunk and smoked in the room we have just occupied, whose young lives were cut short by war. Despite the fact that if he had survived I would never have been born, I weep for their lost love.

So this is how it starts; my curiosity to find out more about my Mother's War, and her desire to record her memories before it is too late.

And what memories they turn out to be.

When we make the decision to record her reminiscences onto tape, we both assume it will be completed in a couple of hours. What she and I anticipate as a couple of foolscap sheets just keeps on coming, page after page, memory after memory.

She is just over fifteen years old and living at The Woodman Hotel when war is declared. Her father's first act is to load a gun with three bullets – one for Pamela, one for his wife and one for himself – and is perfectly reconciled with using it to kill his family if the Germans invade. Pamela accepts that her father knows best without demur.

My mother's life is shaped and reshaped by the war. Her youth is snatched away by circumstances over which she has no control. As she says, 'I was forced to grow up very quickly.' In not much over five short years, she goes from carefree schoolgirl to being a married woman with a baby and an absent husband posted overseas. On the way she enjoys happy times, suffers heartbreaking losses, has a near-death experience, gets married and has a baby, and celebrates when the Second World War finally comes to an end. Her accounts have made me realise why she is the incredible woman that she is today.

This is my mother's story.

This is Pamela's War.

Cherryl Vines, 2012

War is Announced

It is Sunday the 3rd of September 1939. It is not long past eleven in the morning. I am fifteen years and sixteen days old.

The radiogram at my home, The Woodman Hotel in Clent, has just been switched off, the silence resonates around the room, a deathly hush has fallen.

As usual on a Sunday morning the place is full. Weather-worn farm workers lounging in the front bar, dapper businessmen who have escaped the Sunday morning chores to sup a few pints of ale while their long-suffering wives stay at home to prepare the meal. The chef, who wandered out from the hot kitchens just a few minutes ago, wiping his hands on his crisp white apron, is vaguely annoyed that his pre-lunch routine is being disturbed, little knowing how much his life is about to change. The carefree chambermaids have scampered down from their bed-making duties, wondering what on earth can be so important to keep them from their work. My Mother, my Father and I, we are all there to share this terrible piece of news – news that will change our lives forever.

We have all listened to the broadcast in stunned, horrified silence. Although summer is just coming to an end and autumn has barely started, with the golden leaves still stubbornly attached to the trees, there is a chill in the air.

We are in a state of shock, having heard confirmation of news that many have dreaded for months. The Prime

Minister, Neville Chamberlain, has declared that, despite the best efforts of the politicians of the day to secure 'peace in our time', the inevitable has befallen us; despite pledges to the contrary, Germany has invaded Poland, Hitler has ignored requests to back down and so, therefore, 'BRITAIN IS NOW AT WAR WITH GERMANY'.

There is a collective sigh. 'Never mind,' someone says, trying to lighten the mood, 'it'll all be over by Christmas!'

If only! We were not to know it, but there would be six long Christmases of fear, deprivation and shortages before this awful war was over. The Prime Minister has requested that we all play our part with calmness and courage; little do we know at this time just how much courage it will take to get us through this dreadful ordeal.

Minutes after the broadcast ends, my Father, Sidney Wheeler, goes quietly up to his room and prepares for a potentially murderous act.

In a bedroom of the hotel in this quiet Worcestershire village, he methodically loads three bullets into his First World War revolver.

His intention, should the Germans invade, is to shoot his beloved family.

One bullet is for me (Pamela, his only child), the second for his wife Marie (my Mother) and the final one will be used to remove him from the horror of what he has just created through his actions.

He has given this plan a great deal of thought. A veteran of the Somme, he knows the Germans, he knows what is coming, he knows what war does to a man and he sees this act as perfectly reasonable. When the Germans come he will be ready!

Wrapping the loaded weapon carefully in a large cotton handkerchief, he stows it away. Pushing the drawer closed, he turns the key and prays that he will never be forced to have to use it.

Never having experienced the worries and deprivations of war and little knowing what lies ahead, my concerns at this time are rather more focused on my return to school for the new autumn term, getting together my uniform and books and preparing for the forthcoming and dreaded School Certificate.

Though I am not to know it just yet, Herr Hitler is soon to rid me of the requirement for, or the worry of, any of these things.

My Father's War

He has tried hard to put behind him the terrible sights and sounds of the battlefields of the First World War. He rarely speaks about what has happened.

But this 'War to end all Wars' has seen him witness many, many dreadful barbarous acts, including the murder of his best friend, shot through the head by a German leaving a captured bunker. He has never said but I suspect that the perpetrator of this deadly act did not live long after this outrage. He has also witnessed the sickening experience of seeing one of his pals walking beside him who, having stood on a mine, is quite literally blown to kingdom come. There is nothing left of him at all. Absolutely nothing!

And there was so much more.

The rats, the lice, the mud, the blood, the stench of life (and death) in the trenches – most of the troops spending hours up to their knees in water until the command, given by the sound of a whistle, to go over the top to attack – and never knowing who would be next to die. And as if the bombs, the mines and the bullets are not enough of a threat, there is also the terror of mustard gas, which, creeping silently, blinds and kills. When he becomes an Officer he has an additional pressure to deal with. He carries forever the guilt of sending men to their deaths; for making just one wrong call can terminate a life, or many lives, on his say so alone.

The whole vile experience of his war which, together with that of his Birmingham pals, has been entered into with such naïve hope, has culminated in the death of a generation of idealistic young men. They have joined up town-by-town, village-by-village, and since troops are gathered together on a geographical basis, many that fight together die together.

Thus whole villages are robbed of their men – their fathers, sons, brothers and sweethearts; families frequently lose all of the men that they send for sacrifice, as they fight side-by-side – so they die side-by-side.

An entire generation gone forever.

A man does not easily forget these things, or forgive them, EVER.

I think it is true to say that my Father, at this stage in his life, is not terribly fond of the Germans. And never will be.

There are lighter moments in his war, amongst which is the hugely anticipated arrival of the post from home. Without fail, his mother packs and posts a parcel for her darling boy every single week, which arrives without fail every single week, no matter where in Europe he is. The contents of this parcel are consistent and predictable, and one imagines him being teased mercilessly by his fellow soldiers as he unwraps the contents, first revealing the new pair of underpants and then, rolled up inside, the bottle of Lea & Perrins Worcester sauce; the same contents every time. This spicy little bottle of relish proves to be a lifesaver for him since this condiment, when added to the virtually inedible trench rations, makes them almost palatable.

There is naturally also the camaraderie of friends, the sarcastically dark army humour that helps them all get through the unimaginable experiences that war forces upon them. There are also the football matches that take place between the British troops, giving a little light relief in the midst of so much misery, allowing a little normality in the midst of so much madness. He always loved football and won medals for games played as a junior. Sadly for him, the photographs of the time show him in uniform beside his football player troops; he clearly has to settle for reflected glory from now on.

Some time between joining up and his commission, he is temporarily invalided home with rheumatic fever. This is when his lifelong admiration of the Salvation Army begins. For it is they that provide his welcome home from the ship with a cup of tea and a cigarette, a kindness that is never forgotten.

The Incident at
The Midland Hotel

Although he joins up as a private, the war sees my Father promoted quickly through the ranks to Officer status.

This state of affairs could have easily come to a very abrupt end following an incident at a local Birmingham Hotel when he is home on leave. By nature he is a very gentle man, but the war has toughened him up. He is not prepared to put up with any nonsense, not after all the things that he has been forced to witness.

Wearing his very smart dress uniform with its shiny trouser stripes, he is here to relax, but is being loudly harangued by a local 'Hurray Henry' who clearly has chosen not to offer himself up for sacrifice in this Great War when he had the chance, and who has probably consumed far too much alcohol already that evening.

The rude remarks and barracking have continued for some time. My Father has very nearly had enough.

'I say my man are you attending here?' says Henry (for this is what we shall now call him), accompanied by laughter from his equally drunken companions. 'No,' says my Father, incensed at the suggestion that his smart uniform is that of a waiter, 'but I can soon attend to you!' During the ensuing scuffle, Father and Henry struggle next to the open first-floor window of the hotel. Seconds later, much to the horror of the onlookers, my Father's opponent is flying towards his doom on the pavement, well over thirty feet below.

However, it is clearly Henry's lucky day for, instead of crashing to almost certain death or very serious injury on the ground below, he finds himself cradled in the safety of the large awning hanging (happily for him) beneath the window from which he has just been ejected; this breaks his fall and very probably saves his life. Quite how Henry escapes from this canvas cradle is not recorded, for by now my Father is well on his way out of the back door of the building.

The barman, who, having witnessed the whole series of events and whose sympathies clearly lie with my Father, removes him quickly from the scene before he can be identified; an act that probably prevents his war culminating in a rather different conclusion.

Many years after this event, my Father returned to the same hotel and is recognised by the very same barman still working in the bar. They discuss the event, one that has never been forgotten. He confirmed that 'Henry' survived the incident with only his ego damaged: he was considered by all to be a drunken boor who deserved to be taken down a peg or two, and who more than deserved the treatment that he received.

Home from France and Marriage

So by some miracle of fate, my Father returns physically unscathed from the war back to the bosom of his family and his old life in the family business.

The Wheelers have been butchers for decades. They trade from shops in and around the city centre of Birmingham.

Before his war service, he served his apprenticeship from a very early age, learning the cuts, preparation and storage of meat. He also acts as delivery boy. As a very young boy he is asked to deliver an order of steak to a local theatre. It is for the prima ballerina Anna Pavlova, who is on a tour of the country and is performing in Birmingham for a few nights.

He arrives on his bicycle. For his trouble his prize is a meeting with the beautiful dancer and the reward of a florin, a 2-shilling piece, which she presses into his hand as a tip. He has this precious keepsake for many years until it is stolen.

*

During wartime leave he has met my mother, Marie. One of three children, she is pretty, vivacious and fun to be with. Her sister Edith, from whom I inherit my much-detested middle name, is a talented musician; she frequently plays and sings for the BBC. They have a younger brother, Fred. This much-awaited son and heir is a happy arrival after the birth of two girls, but the entire family spoil him – a fact that probably shapes his behaviour as an adult, which sometimes leaves a little to be desired. Towards the middle of his life, my Father has grown to detest him. He bans him from the house, but my Mother adores her little brother and feels he can do no wrong.

Apart from her delightful personality and her good looks, Marie is also a very skilled seamstress; she has served an apprenticeship as a milliner with Madame De Leats in Edgbaston and is capable of creating and making the most beautiful hats. She charms everyone with whom she comes in contact.

It is not long before Sidney proposes and she accepts.

He has survived the war and this is the start of the rest of his life.

It is Monday, July the 10th, 1922 when they marry at St Peter's Church in the village of Harborne, and their guests are driven en masse in a charabanc the fifteen miles to The Tontine, a hotel on the River Severn at Stourport, for the wedding breakfast. Quite an adventure!

They set up home together in accommodation over the butcher's shop in Harborne High Street. This was then, as now, a vibrant and busy trading area. The days are long; with very early starts necessitated by the trips for buying meat at the market in the Bull Ring, but the business is successful, which, given the expensive tastes of my Grandfather, who works and lives with them, is just as well.

He is a very dapper dresser and insists that all his clothes (including his vests) be handmade. Only the best will do!

A New Arrival

I have, by now, entered the world, born on August the 18th 1924 at a local nursing home. I grow into a serious, dark-skinned and brown-eyed child with straight brown hair. Greatly cherished by all the family, my Mother treats me rather like a large doll. I am in possession of the most beautiful wardrobe of clothes and shoes, including a white fur coat with a matching hat: everything to coordinate. I look so very smart!

Since I am an only child, I am doted on, indulged and a little spoilt. I usually demand (and get) my own way!

The lady, whose role (and possible misfortune) it is to care for me during the day, is subjected to my favourite pastime. I love nothing better than to sink my little baby teeth into her arm as deep as I can go.

When my straight hair does not conform to the fashion of the day, and given my Mother's desire to be the parent of a curly-haired moppet, I am forced to undergo a number of frightening and smelly sessions with the curling tongues. Heated on the stove over the open gas flame, the temperature control of which leaves everything to be desired, my small ears sometimes get in the way of this vile equipment. I hate it!

I really do not want to be curly that much! Furthermore, the tongues offer curls of only a temporary nature – they soon drop out and my hair returns to its natural straight state.

Undaunted in her desire to achieve her view of physical perfection for me, I am later introduced, as a very small child, to the hairdressers and the misery and chemicals of permanent waves. 'Perms', which equally disgust my young nostrils but do offer a more permanent result for those determined that I have curls, and curls I do have!

At around three years of age, and probably much to the relief of my well-bitten carer, she is offered some respite when I am sent to a small private nursery in the village. Within the first few days, finding it not much to my liking I return home alone. On another occasion I recruit a willing cohort and I am able to navigate both of us over several busy roads to the local park, which strikes me at the time as being much more like fun than school! Everyone, including the police and neighbours, are in full cry when we are both finally located, playing on the swings, none the worse for our adventure.

New Directions

By now my Father has become aware of the clout that his wife's father has in the pub trade locally. His father-in-law, Arthur James, is in charge of all licensed premises in the area, on behalf of a large local brewery called Mitchells and Butlers. It is an important role as he has the say over which pubs are allocated and to whom.

By a strange coincidence, the linking of the two trades of butchery and beer stretches back centuries, butcher's shops frequently being situated on the same site as public houses. (Indeed my own great-great-grandfather was born in a room above a butcher's shop situated in the Crown at Deritend, the oldest pub in Birmingham.)

So now he can change direction, he has a means of entry into the world of pubs and brewing and the possibility of a new career path, should he want one.

For an ambitious young man with a young family, this is too good an opportunity to ignore. After a few years of marriage, he and my Mother start to contemplate the possibility of a life in the licensed trade. Here is a chance for them to move to the country, run their own business and work for themselves, together as a family.

So the young couple decide that this is the time to practice their entrepreneurial skills, and they take the lease on a small village pub in Hagley called the Prince of Wales. The butcher's shop (situated on the outskirts of Birmingham) is soon dropped in favour of the pub, as the commute between the two premises and the early starts required by the meat market prove to be too difficult.

I attend the local village school and, apart from longing for a brother or sister for company (neither of which appear), I enjoy a carefree childhood.

The pub is soon a great success and after a few years of trading in Hagley they realise that, since they both love this new life, and with my Father's business acumen and my Mother's love of entertaining and her skills with people, that they have found their calling in life. However, both can see even greater rewards offered by larger premises where they could have letting bedrooms, lunches, dinners, bed and breakfast. So when the opportunity arises, almost certainly aided by the intervention of my maternal Grandfather Arthur, they decide to take the lease on a hotel in the next village of Clent. This is where I find myself at the beginning of this story.

My Dog Bonzo

Possibly to soften the news of a move to a new location (children being notoriously averse to change), I am first promised and then presented with a dog. He is a little brown terrier puppy, and his name is Bonzo. He becomes my very best friend; he sleeps on my bed and we become inseparable.

Shortly after his arrival into the family, we very nearly lose him to distemper, a serious illness in puppies, but he is saved with alcohol. My Father administers brandy and advocaat. It takes time but he recovers and thrives.

A local dog owner, hearing about this miracle cure and having a puppy allegedly suffering from the same ailment (which generally proves fatal), is offered the same cure and it works for him too!

My little dog very reluctantly allows me out of his sight to catch the morning bus to school and is always waiting for me on my return. However, in my absence, his days are not wasted. He has a lovely life. He ventures forth and makes friends with the local canine population. Rumour has it that in the fullness of time, many puppies with features and colouring resembling Bonzo begin to appear in the local neighbourhood.

His highly questionable morals include a tendency towards kleptomania. There is a small shop next door to our hotel and Bonzo regularly helps himself to the walnuts, which are on display outside. He then runs off with his prize, taking them to a quiet place to crunch

his way through his stolen snack. When these are
consumed, he creeps back to replenish his supply. Our
grocer neighbour, struggling to make a living, as we all
are, points out that Bonzo is eating what little profit he
has. The nuts are relocated out of the dog's reach.

He is a very bright dog and he understands every
word that is said to him. One day, as my Mother is about
to take her afternoon nap, she tells Bonzo to 'go and get
Mummy a chookie.'

This ruse, meant to get him out of her room to enable
her to sleep, backfires in a spectacular way.

Before long, a large white chicken is laid ceremoniously
on the lawn outside her bedroom window. It is indeed a
chookie; but it is a very dead chookie!

Before we can stop him, Bonzo has added a further
three chickens to this cache! He has obeyed her
instructions to the letter. Fourfold!

It costs my Father the price of the four chickens, many
sincere apologies and reassurances that Bonzo will never
do such a thing ever again in order to pacify Mr Coles,
the owner of the chookies. We dare not admit that our
loyal dog was only following orders. But how clever was
he to understand and follow instructions like that. What
a dog!

Bonzo is a dog of few scruples. Despite there being
more than enough for him to eat in the hotel kitchens,
he delights in parting people from their food, however
meagre their rations; it seems the more needy they are
the better he likes it. So one afternoon he hones in on a
poor old chap who has taken his lunch break in the front
bar of the hotel. This man has with him a very modest
lunch tied up in a cloth Dick Whittington-style and a
rusty old knife with which to cut it up. He has limited
bread and a very small amount of cheese but Bonzo puts
on his prima donna performance: he sits on his hind legs

whimpers and begs, his little face so appealing and sad as if he has not eaten for a month. He succeeds in his ploy and parts the man from the lion's share of his lunch. Not much better than stealing but at least on this occasion he is obliged to sing for his supper.

So Bonzo really does have a dog's life, several canine lady friends in close proximity, delicious snacks available whenever he feels peckish and his very favourite pastime; rides in the car. It takes only one or two blasts of the car horn and no matter how far from home he has ventured, he appears wagging his little tail, ready for a trip out. He loves shopping!

I adore this dog and could never imagine being parted from him.

In time, the war will take him away from me, as it will do to so many of those I love.

The Cricket Team

Just after our move to the hotel, I am flattered to find myself in demand from the local boys who play cricket on the field opposite. The door is frequently knocked in the early afternoons of the summer holidays and the enquiry made to my Father about my availability to come out to play cricket.

Happy for me to have young company, fresh air and exercise, my Father agrees that it is a very good idea for me to go out to play.

For my own part, I am delighted to join in the game and so I spend much of that summer listening to the sound of ball on willow. It is lovely to be so popular!

However, it is not too long before the truth behind my popularity sinks in.

When I return home from my game one afternoon, my Father has enquired whether I prefer to bat or bowl and I have to tell him that since I have never been asked to take up either of these roles, I have absolutely no idea!

I realise that I am always given the same position in the game; I only ever get to play fielder, way out on the boundary.

I am the only one running back and forth to get the ball. Every one else (that is to say the boys) always get to play the game with the bat or the ball and they never, ever have to field.

Well why would they when there's an innocent, stupid girl running round for them!

I NEVER, EVER get asked to bat or to bowl.
I AM BEING USED!
Enough is enough!
I am suddenly unavailable.
They can chase their own ball!

A Successful Venture

So the hotel plans progress. With six letting bedrooms, a bar, a lounge and a large upstairs room soon to be converted to an exclusive dining room, the number of staff appointed eventually reaches fourteen, to include chefs, chambermaids, waiters, cleaners and a kitchen porter; we even have a peak-capped car park attendant for the newly floodlit car park. This is going to be the place to be seen!

My Father is very good friends with theatre owners in the area, so it is not long before the clientele include famous members of the acting and entertainment fraternity who, appearing at these local theatres, seek the relative solitude of the countryside between performances. Tommy Trinder, performing in *Why Go to Paris* in Wolverhampton, is one of the many famous stars of the day who spend time under our roof. For someone of my age it is all very exciting!

Before long the car park is full of the top of the range vehicles of the day. The local car club from Hagley have started to meet here for a 'noggin and a natter', and on their meet nights the car park is full of earnest-looking young men with a pint of beer in one hand and a cigarette or pipe in the other, staring, fascinated, into the open bonnets of each of the cars. This is now most definitely the place to be seen!

Cocktails are the order of the day and so a stylish cocktail bar is designed downstairs. Chrome and mirror are in abundance. Upstairs, a dining room is created with a smart black, flame and gold colour scheme, utilising Lloyd Loom chairs set around small round tables with a central dance floor. Music is piped up from the radiogram in the bar below. Three large, open fireplaces with blazing fires create a warm and welcoming atmosphere during the cold winter months.

My parents are convinced that this is a great career move – they will make their fortune! How can they fail? The Depression is over; it is all going swimmingly well; optimism is in the air; what can possibly go wrong?

They cannot start to imagine how the plans and actions of a short, moustachioed Austrian, already busy hundreds of miles away in Germany building the foundations of the Third Reich, will eventually impact on their lives and business.

Learning to Dance

In the dining room upstairs, there is a small dance floor and it is here that I am taught to dance by a couple of gentlemen friends of my Mother's. They are quite an odd pairing, one very thin and the other extremely rotund and, looking back now, I would guess that this rather effete couple might well have been more than dancing partners. They teach me well and I am soon able to waltz, quickstep and cha-cha-cha with confidence. These lessons have to be carried out in secret as technically, at only fourteen years of age, this room, with its license to sell intoxicating liquor, is strictly out of bounds to me. But since the dance music is piped from the bar below where my Father is busy, whenever he is out of sight and my teachers are visiting, I am able to practise my skills.

Jack the barman is always on hand to shout a warning should my Father reappear, at which point I can scamper back to my bedroom. He is none the wiser.

In future years I will be grateful for these dancing skills, when I am able to dance the night away!

Royal Secrets and the King's Speech

Before the war starts, one of our regular early evening customers is a man who, living locally, enjoys dropping in on weeknights after work for a pre-dinner drink. He does not want me or Jack the barman around when this aperitif is prepared; he is here for the conversation as much as the alcohol and requests particularly that my Father be available to prepare his pink gins and have a chat. My Father complies willingly; he too relishes the intelligent conversations and repartee that he has with this gentleman. Their chats are sometimes very revealing.

Our customer enjoys unwinding after the stresses of the day; he has a very senior job with the family of the local land-owning aristocracy.

They mix with royalty.

He has insider knowledge.

The gin lowers his reserve a little (though he knows the information will go no further).

So it is he who shares with my Father the fears of those in power regarding the hold that an American divorcee seems to have over our future king – a fact that has been kept from the British people by the Press, who have been very efficiently gagged. We are kept completely in the dark. It is some years before we, the general public, get to know more about Wallis Simpson and when we realise the implications of the romance and hear Edward confirm that he cannot continue without the help and support of the woman he loves beside him, we fear that all is lost. Our handsome and debonair Prince is reluctant to fulfil his destiny. Not long after this, we change the words of the carol and that Christmas we sing, 'Hark the Herald angels sing, Mrs Simpson stole our King'.

My Father's companion also voices the very real concerns of those 'in the know' regarding the Prince's younger brother Bertie. He suffers from an appalling speech impediment, is barely able to string a sentence together, has nothing of the charisma of his older brother and is simply not up to the job of King. If Edward is not prepared to be King, how on earth can his shy, stuttering and unprepared younger brother do the job?

We realise later, however, that he is going to have to fulfil this role whether he likes it or not! And as time will show, he makes a pretty good job of it.

Light Fingers

Although the employment of staff helps to spread the heavy workload at the hotel, they sometimes create as many problems as they are there to solve.

Some prove to be more than a little light-fingered.

One girl, a cleaner called Ann, is quitting the hotel following a dispute with my Father over the quality of her work; she has been given the sack. One of her tasks was to keep the silverware cleaned and polished. Having been living in, she is in the hall, just about to leave. She is a generously proportioned young lady and she has a very large suitcase with her, which she is struggling to lift. It appears to be very heavy. Suspiciously so. 'Before you go anywhere,' says my Father, 'I want to see inside your suitcase.'

'Absolutely not!' says Ann.

'If you do not open that suitcase now,' says my Father, 'I am going across the road to the police station and Sergeant Clarke will open it for you!'

So, reluctantly, very reluctantly, she opens her case and there hidden amongst her few clothes is almost the entire silver collection of the hotel. The threat of police involvement is enough; the silver is promptly removed from her possession and she leaves.

Another member of staff, having secreted a packet of cigarettes in the top of her stocking (quite a good hiding place I thought), could never have guessed that her crime would come to light when she was dancing just a little too energetically. When she lifts her skirts a fraction too high, I have spotted the cigarettes snuggled up against her thigh and report this fact back to my Father. 'How on earth could you know?' she says when challenged and forced to hand back the stolen goods. 'I have my informers,' says my Father.

Other classic hiding places for money taken from the till (or not making it in there in the first place) include the front of blouses and down the sides of shoes. We have our eyes peeled at all times as, sadly, few of them prove to be trustworthy.

The turquoise ring given to me by my Grandmother is stolen from my room. My Fathers treasured florin, the one given to him by Pavlova, goes the same way. We lose lots of small treasured possessions but it is difficult to keep everything under lock and key. And we can trust no one.

It is not just the members of staff that need watching. Someone reports to my Father that one of the Lloyd Loom chairs from the cocktail lounge is being loaded into the back of a car in the car park.

'Have you just sold one?'

'No I bloody well have not!'

Only swift action prevents it being driven off to a new home elsewhere. It is removed from the car and returned to its rightful place.

Perhaps it is the shortages of war, but light fingers do seem to be the order of the day!

One afternoon I notice a young woman passing my open bedroom door, which is on the first floor. She is not a guest of the hotel, nor a member of staff, nor a customer. Indeed, I have never seen her before. When I look again I realise that this stranger is wearing a very smart hat, which looks remarkably familiar. It closely resembles the navy blue osprey-trimmed hat that my

Mother was wearing on our shopping trip earlier that day. Having taken it off on our return, she had put it on the bed of her unlocked bedroom. It is a lovely hat of which she is justly proud! Osprey feathers are very expensive. This is a very special hat!

It is indeed my Mother's hat!

When challenged, the girl makes a run for it, going swiftly down the stairs and out of the front door, up the lane and away; presumably she has an accomplice waiting in a car. Neither she nor the hat is ever seen again! Its loss is lamented for years.

Day Trippers

The Clent Hills, always a good venue for fresh air and fun, have become an increasingly popular holiday spot for the workers from Lye, an industrial area close to Stourbridge. There are many factories here and the housing is of poor quality; money is tight, seaside holidays out of the question.

Arriving on double-decker buses, this day out promises to be a great adventure for them all; men, women and children. Many roll off the bus straight into the front bar, proceed to get very drunk and don't even make it up onto the Clent Hills for the fresh air and exercise, supposedly the true reason for the visit. The children are not allowed into the hotel and are forced to sit patiently in the garden with crisps and lemonade; this can sometimes be a very long and tedious wait.

It is a fifteen-minute walk from where we are up onto the Hills. There are ponies here, which can be hired for half an hour for a little trek around the pony ring.

No previous riding experience is required, these little ponies know their way round without guidance – they can do it blindfolded. The biggest risk to the novice rider on the return journey, however, is being able to stay on board. Lulled into a false sense of security during the slow amble up the hill, the riders are forced to hang on for grim death for, from the very moment the pony rounds the last corner and catches sight of home and realises there might be a possibility of food, or a rest, the slow amble turns into a trot, a notoriously difficult pace for a novice. It is very easy to get bumped off. Many ponies get rid of their unwanted cargoes on the home run and return home alone!

Those that do make it up the hill – who have an inclination for drink – can sample the beverages on sale at two other pubs, The Hill Tavern and The Fountain Inn. We are the last in line before the bus home, so those that have enjoyed a tipple elsewhere are highly inebriated by the time they get to us!

When drunk they behave very badly, some dance on the tables and the really unruly ones are so out of control that they have to be arrested by the local policeman and kept over night in the cells to cool off.

Another visitor from Lye, both before and during the war, is the vegetable man. He arrives once a week with his horse and cart loaded with fresh vegetables, brown paper bags and a set of scales balanced precariously on the back. Touring the lanes, he stops at cottages and houses in the nearby villages to sell his produce. His final stop at the end of the day is our hotel. It is here that most of the day's profits are spent on beer – and plenty of it.

As a consequence, at closing time he is unable to get back onto his cart without help! He is very drunk!

Undaunted, several of his front bar companions give him a leg up, settle him in his seat, make sure that he is facing towards home, put the reins in his hands, smack the horse on the rear and off they go. His horse, rather like the ponies on Clent, knows the way home, though in his case it is much further all the way back to Lye – over four miles away! We are confident of this fact when he reappears without harm the following week, when the whole exercise is repeated.

New Friends

As an only child, although greatly loved by both of my parents and despite the company of my lovely little dog, I am rather lonely. Returning from school to silent premises, it is often the chef providing the company and chat with a cup of tea that in normal households Mum or Dad would be around to proffer. Mine are resting. This afternoon nap is sacrosanct. Maybe they are sleeping off the excesses of lunchtime or, more likely, recharging batteries for the forthcoming evening. Whichever, I am left to entertain myself.

Around this time I have become friendly with the children of one of the customers of the hotel. Their father is a successful local businessman. The family consists of a girl, Gloria, aged twelve, a little younger than my fourteen-year-old self, and her twin sisters, who are aged about ten.

Theirs is such a sad story; their mother has abandoned them, left her life of wealth and privilege, left her beautiful home, her lovely children, abandoned her stunned husband; she is a bolter. She has run off with a man from the railway. How could she do this? This act has shaken the family to its very core.

The family have moved into the hotel while their father establishes a new home for them all. The two younger girls are shortly to be sent to boarding school in Malvern; Gloria will carry on at Red Hill School in Stourbridge to provide continuity in her education.

Being an only child, I relish the company of this instant little family and form a bond of friendship that is to last a lifetime. This is a truly joyful time for me. This family are well-travelled and wealthy and they introduce me to many of the wonderful and cultured things of life; with them I attend Shakespeare plays at Stratford, develop a lifelong love of opera, enjoy the excitement of fast, open-topped cars and learn to relish the taste of both champagne and oysters. There would seem to be no age restrictions on either!

The Motor Car

Although we attend different schools in the same local market town and, despite the age gap, Gloria and I have become the very best of friends. Around this time (indulged one might say) she is presented with a convertible motorcar.

It seems hard to imagine now that a girl of only thirteen years of age could be given a sports car and be allowed to drive unsupervised (if you don't count my involvement, and, as a fifteen year old, I have not a clue as to the workings of the internal combustion engine nor the rules of the road). But at this time it is not necessary to take or pass a driving test, although you are meant to have a licence and to have attained the necessary number of years (a small oversight in our case). So all that is necessary to get moving is to get in, master the controls and drive! So that is exactly what my best friend does, with me sitting beside her. She has to park around the corner from the hotel because we both know that Father will not countenance me being driven by one so young. But that is not enough to stop us!

So, one sunny morning I have walked down the lane and round the corner, jumped into the car and off we go! We are heading towards Stourbridge, our local market town; the car roof is down so we are relishing the joys of the open road, the sun in our eyes, and the wind in our hair. Bliss! But suddenly there is a rude awakening. I look up and spot my Father coming in the opposite direction; he has been to the bank to collect change for the weeks' trading. He is in my Mother's car, in the passenger seat of the oncoming vehicle (never having learned to drive), and Jack the barman is at the wheel. Instead of ducking down to avoid recognition, I cry out, 'Oh look there's Dad!' and wave frantically at him and he waves back; it is a completely spontaneous reaction. We both smile but goodness knows why, for this is not a matter for joy or laughter. We both realise with horror (mine probably greater than his) the implication of this greeting as the gap between the two vehicles increases. But I can do nothing, it is too late, the deed is done. My Father is very protective of me and quite controlling; we are probably about to be in big trouble.

Which indeed we are.

Very, very big trouble.

We get as far as Hagley. There is a policeman waiting for us by the side of the road.

We are stopped.

'Miss Wheeler?'

'Yes.'

'Miss Eveson?'

'Yes.'

'What are you doing driving this motorcar?'

'My Daddy gave it to me.'

'Just remind me, how old are you?'

'Thirteen.'

'But you are not old enough to drive! Take it home now and do not attempt to take it out again until you are old enough!'

Severely chastened, we return the car to Pedmore. It remains there for quite a time.

Clearly, following our encounter on the road, my Father has dashed straight to the police station in Clent, a swift phone call has been made and the Hagley officer has leapt to attention just in time to stop us.

And so ended our motoring days.

Cigarettes, Ice Cream and Coffee

Forced to travel by bus, since our wheels have been confiscated, Gloria and I meet every Saturday in the local market town of Stourbridge.

Our first stop on reaching town is to the tobacconists. It is a very adult place, dark and mysterious, and we relish its deliciously sweet, heady tobacco odours. It is here that we purchase a packet of Turkish cigarettes. These seem to us to be the epitome of sophistication but they are incredibly difficult to smoke and almost impossible to inhale; the tobacco is very strong and it burns our throats as we struggle to smoke them. There are no restrictions as to where we are allowed to practice our new skills; we are able to smoke in the restaurant, the cinema and the ice-cream parlour. We do not know at the time but these cigarettes will lead Gloria to a lifelong nicotine addiction, which in time will shorten her life.

Although my Father, too, is a heavy smoker, a habit started in the trenches of the first war – he is rarely seen without a cigarette clutched between his teeth (which shortens his life also) – I prefer to keep my new habit secret from him.

A light lunch in Cranages, a restaurant in the High Street, with its amazing, curved-glass window frontage, is followed by a visit to the local cinema, where we watch the current film. We then walk down the High Street to the local bookshop to buy the novel on which the film is based, every word of which is to be relished during the following weeks. We cast ourselves as the heroines of Mandalay and the Tara plantation house. Rebecca and Scarlet O'Hara. We are at the perfect age for romantic dreams.

The book purchase is generally followed by a visit to the local Italian coffee shop and ice-cream parlour, which we call Googleomo's. I have no idea how this name came about; perhaps it was cast on the front of the big, chrome coffee machine that frothed and gurgled its delicious contents into our cups, or perhaps it is our take on an unpronounceable Italian name. Whichever, it was here that we would often meet up with Gloria's cousin, Geoff. Slightly older than both of us, he is employed in his family butchery business. He is a very good-looking young man and he and I become good friends. This friendship extends to letter writing throughout the early years of his war service. This continues until his capture, after which no further letters appear.

I keep his last letter to me and am able to return it to him when he is finally freed and we meet up as adults.

Sadly for him, his ultimate fate, after enlisting and serving some years as an Officer in the Far East, is to end up in the hands of the Japanese, whose cruelty to their prisoners knows no bounds.

While imprisoned, he and some comrades have been allocated the task of herding the cattle on one of the long, forced marches, and are able to steal a couple of cows. Along the way, two of the cattle are rustled by their keepers, who are able to convince their captors that the missing beasts have suffered from a serious disease which would make them dangerous for human consumption. But in reality, only the horns and hooves are buried, the meat goes into the bellies of the ravenous captives. Geoff's butchery skills are put to good use. This theft preserves quite a few lives for a while longer.

Fortunately (and goodness knows how or why), they are never found out.

His treatment at the hands of the Japanese is despicable. He and his fellow Prisoners of War are all but starved to death; most are brutalised and many are murdered, often on a whim. When I meet him later in life and am able to return his last letter, I am unable to recognise any of the features of the handsome young man of the past. Not one element of his former self is there. The ordeal has broken him, as it has his fellow survivors; it has changed him beyond all recognition and it will eventually lead to his premature death.

But we know nothing of the future that awaits any of us. We are young and carefree and in a place where they serve the VERY BEST coffee and the VERY BEST ice cream in the world.

Not long after the war starts, poor Googleomo has the glass in every window of his shop smashed because he is an Italian and the local population don't now want Italians in their town, however good the ice cream. Shortly after this he is imprisoned, joining his fellow Italians in an internment camp, because by now the Italians have entered the war and are now our enemy.

So ends our coffee and ice cream.

A New Hobby

By now, an old cricketing companion from my earliest days in Clent has re-entered my field of vision; his previous exploitation of my good nature is now history. I have forgiven him. Still living nearby in the village, he has grown older and is now quite handsome. Gloria and I, having just noticed this and having time on our hands, decide that his pursuit can be our new hobby!

He is now a chorister at the local church.

If we are to see him we will need to become part of the Church family.

We must find God!

So, whenever possible, we attend church. Is the vicar thrilled at the increase in his congregation, or has he seen it before, this flowering interest in Jesus by girls of a certain age?

We feel our involvement should go beyond just church attendance.

There are no vacancies in the choir. But bell ringers are required. It can't be that difficult, surely?

What a perfect thing to do. I have always enjoyed being musical. The idea of creating melodic, metallic, chimes to celebrate the passing of the church year seems very attractive.

Christenings, marriages, funerals, Christmas, Easter – they will all require our input to mark their passing.

We will need to be there often; we will have plenty of opportunities to bump into our quarry.

This is a great plan!

Our first disappointment comes when we realise we will not see our young man on our rehearsal night, the sound of the bells not being compatible with choral practise.

The second is that the other bell ringers are really quite old.

Also, the bell tower is cold and spidery and a bit scary. Bell ringing is very noisy and it isn't half as easy as we thought. Our bell-ringing career is short-lived; we will have to find other ways to meet boys.

In any event, our skills would not be required for very long, since, once war is declared, the ringing of church bells is banned.

They are to be rung only in the event of an invasion.

A sound that, in these circumstances, absolutely no one wants to hear.

18

Horse Riding with a Comedian

As well as passing the weekends in the company of my good friend Gloria, I also have grown-ups for company, amongst whom are 'Uncle' Alf Joseph and his wife 'Auntie' Leah. They are childless and he takes me under his wing. The Josephs are close family friends and very kind. This generosity will extend to providing my whole family with refuge at a later stage in this story.

It is Alf who takes me to the local riding school, paying for lessons and teaching me all he knows about horses and, later, accompanying me on hacks around the lanes and bridle paths in the area.

After a few months of lessons, getting 'my seat', learning to rise to the trot and understanding how to control my little mount, I am quite a confident rider.

Our hacks from Stakenbridge take us across a large grass meadow before we reach any roads and this is where we let both horse and pony have their heads. We go like the wind! My little mare is fast and feisty, and, despite her having much shorter legs than Uncle Alf's 17-hand horse, when we gallop she keeps up really well and I often win the race.

On one occasion, one of the hotel's more famous guests, Max Wall, a comedian famed for his strange appearance and funny walk, who is blessed with the same sense of humour both on and off stage, insists that it is high time he joined us on one of our rides.

The fact that he has no previous riding experience is not a consideration.

Most non-riders assume that horse riding involves no skill or training whatsoever; they have seen the cowboy films – it looks so easy, you just get on and go! (This is obviously not true.) Although neither Alf nor I relish the idea of an intruder on our ride, since Max is an honoured (and famous) guest, we feel that we must indulge him.

And so, one sunny Sunday morning, we arrive at the stables and a suitably sized mount is selected for Max.

He has already made the action of getting onto his horse a moment for high jinks; everyone watching is tickled to death by his antics. He is a very funny man!

We leave the stables and enter the meadow.

Our galloping meadow.

Horses are creatures of habit; our two know that this is the place where they can have a good race and when one goes they all go! They enjoy going at full pelt and, with the bit between their teeth, they can be very difficult to stop. The fact that this might happen has not occurred to either Alf or myself.

As our mounts take off, so, of course, does the one that Max is riding. He is hanging on for grim death, and shouting loudly, 'The brakes! The brakes! Where are the brakes? How do you stop the bloody thing? Where the hell are the brakes? HELP!'

By the time we manage to pull our mounts to a halt, which in turn stops his, he has just about managed to stay on. But he is out of the saddle and hanging round the neck of his horse, very close to its ears. He looks funnier than ever!

He lets Alf know that since he got no pleasure whatsoever from his first – and last – equestrian experience, he will not be joining us next Sunday, 'thank you very much'. We help him off (he's halfway off already) and, leading our horses, we walk in silence back across our galloping meadow and return our mounts to the stables.

Alf and I are both quietly relieved that our Sunday hacks will remain exclusive to us from now on.

19

The Water Otter

Alf has a well-developed sense of humour and I am often the sidekick and assistant for his practical jokes.

On one occasion he sets up a scenario, which involves parting many of the customers (his friends) from half a crown of their money each. The elaborate hoax first involves the starting of a rumour that a very rare creature had been spotted locally. This story then develops. The creature has been captured and will be put on display and anyone wishing to view will be obliged to pay. With his skills as a showman, Alf is able to whip up the level of excitement Posters are produced. The cry goes up. 'Roll up! Roll up! Come and see this rare creature!'

And so a queue forms outside the greenhouse where the creature is held. What has he captured?

An otter.

A water otter.

A rare creature indeed!

I collect the money. The half crowns mount up. The viewing public are obliged to enter through one door and leave through another, lest they share with their fellow punters the disappointing news that they were being charged to view an enormous black kettle which, it has to be said, without argument, is most definitely the biggest water hotter in the county. Everyone takes it in good part. I think the view of all those hoaxed is that it is a clever and amusing trick and worth the money (which goes to charity) for the entertainment value.

So my pre-war years pass happily; little do I know what lies ahead.

20

Shopping

Before the war starts, and happily before the time of rationing and shortages, Mother and I enjoy frequent shopping trips to Birmingham. We pile into her little Austin car early in the morning and off we go. Bonzo invariably accompanies us.

He loves the car.

We love the shops.

Bonzo, truly content just to have been allowed to travel in the car, stays patiently waiting for us, and whilst provided with fresh air, water and food, he usually chooses to sleep soundly until our return.

Birmingham, at this time, is a marvellous place to shop. Lewis's, Greys and Marshall, and Snelgrove are our favourite department stores. They have everything that we could possibly need. There are also many independent milliners and shoe shops. Mother takes great pleasure in spoiling me, buying me lots of lovely things. It is a precious time for both of us. The business of running the hotel is very time-consuming, so it is good to spend some special time together.

Occasionally, Father joins us to patronise his favourite gentleman's outfitters, Morgan and Ball. It is from here that he purchases his trademark trilby hats and Crombie overcoats.

He is never seen out without his trilby hat.

We usually arrive back laden with bags of clothes and shoes. Although we are not to know it, this wardrobe of clothes and shoes that we are laying down will have to last us for the duration of the war, and beyond. As coupons are introduced, we need to be very much more circumspect with our purchases. Soon it will require an entire year's worth of clothing coupons just to purchase a winter coat.

Leaving School

I attend the local Girls' High School in Stourbridge, for which my Father is obliged to pay fees. I am not particularly interested in the academic side of school but I do enjoy being creative. However, when I return one afternoon with a pipe – which I have lovingly fashioned myself from a piece of wood during a music lesson – he queries, quite loudly, what on earth his money is paying for? Indeed, he is sufficiently annoyed, much to my embarrassment, to present himself at school the next morning to address this question to the mistress concerned. The money spent on fees is soon of no consequence, however, for, as the war starts, the hotel staff are called up, and given that there is no air-raid shelter available at school, I am permitted to leave without the need to sit any exams (hurrah!) and I am allowed to start working behind the cocktail bar, a concession, given my young age, that requires special permission from both the brewery and the local police.

In the circumstances, I do not have an interview for my new job. Instead, Mr Bob Butler, one of the brewery directors, who lives nearby, comes and tests my mathematical skills by ordering several rounds of drinks. Clearly I come up to his expectations and the job is mine!

The Germans on the Hill

Petrol becomes limited almost immediately when war is declared; the rules applying to its use are draconian.

So, with fewer and fewer customers able to drive and very few within walking distance, what customers we do have become the focus of considerably more attention than they would previously have received.

This is probably why a group of men who have begun arriving early in the evening attract the attention of my Father.

They arrive in a small group having meandered down the lane directly opposite the hotel; the lane leading to the hills. There are a number of properties up here, including a very large house, which we understand to be operating as a nursing home. They also grow and sell a large range of vegetables, which are raised in the extensive grounds, and some of this produce is sold to the local public. Surrounded by fields at the front, its grounds back tightly up to a heavily wooded section of the Clent Hills at the rear.

The men arrive at the same time each evening, ordering their drinks in English and then sitting and talking quietly in their Mother tongue. My Father stands behind the bar, struggling to identify this foreign language. He listens carefully.

Though not extensively travelled (apart from his war service), he knows that he has heard this language before. He remembers his time in France – his time on the Somme – and this guttural sound does seem very familiar. But this is not French that he is catching the odd word of. He strains really hard, and then he realises.

With a burst of adrenalin and fury, he realises that these men are the Hun, the Germans! His old enemy! What on earth can they be doing in a small Worcestershire village several months into the war?

So when the leader arrives to order the next round of drinks he is ready.

'You are German?' asks my Father.

'I am!'

'I fought against your lot on the Somme.'

'Me too. I probably took a pot shot at you!'

'And,' says my Father; 'I probably took a pot shot at you too!'

The exchange over, the man pays for his drinks and returns to his friends, carrying on with their conversation.

My Father recognises his old enemy.

He is more than ready to deal with him.

They are from the big house up the lane, no doubt about that. So I am recruited to find out exactly what is happening there. Absolutely fearless, I am the heroine of this adventure! Under the pretext of buying vegetables, I wander up to the house and ring the doorbell, and, whilst my potatoes and carrots are being fetched, I am counting the number of people walking around inside; there are so many of them! Where have they all come from? I report back to Father all that I have seen.

I am able to repeat this action on several occasions before I am told, by those that open the door to me, that under no circumstances am I to come up to the house again; I must make my purchases from the shop in the lane. I can do no more. What does this ban signify; do they have something to hide?

I now doubt very much that my clandestine counting of heads added anything to the sum total of knowledge at the time, or indeed went anyway to altering the outcome of the war. But I do like to think that I was ready when called.

The concerns regarding 'the enemy within' are now reaching new heights. A German maid working for an elderly lady in a house on the hills is seen opening and closing curtains at night. Despite being warned to stop, she continues the practise, and is promptly jailed. It is also noted that one of the large, flat roofs at the big house seems recently to have been painted white; could this be a sign for the bombers that are nightly pounding the nearby cities and aircraft factories? Could it be a marker to allow the enemy to parachute in at the dead of night? We are all on high alert!

Since my Father is by now leading the local Home Guard battalion, he uses his influence to report the fact that we have a group of Germans nearby whom he believes to be a cause for concern. The Home Office is contacted post haste, their action is prompt and it is not long before hoards of police cars scream past the front of the hotel and tear up the lane to the big house.

It concerns me slightly from this distance in time that many of these poor people about to be parted from their freedom, for no other reason than their country of birth, could have been working quite legitimately, motivated by the very best of intentions. They may well have numbered Jews amongst them, who would have despised Hitler as much as we did. But then, as now, the law wields a broad brush and not long after this, I am standing in a crowd of jeering and fist-shaking villagers on the front of the hotel, as the Germans are driven away to be imprisoned. We are all very happy at this outcome.

History records that what you, dear reader, may consider to be the worst kind of racist paranoia was, in part at least, well founded.

Very many years later, I attend a Land Army reunion in Worcester and meet someone from Pershore. On discovering where I was based during the war she says, 'Oh yes, I remember hearing about Clent – that was where my father (a policeman from Lye) was sent to inspect a nursing home, and he found radio transmitters up the chimneys!'

Make of that what you will.

23

Family Rows

Working and living together for twenty-four hours a day, seven days a week, puts an enormous strain on even the strongest of relationships. But throw alcohol, two strong, feisty characters and an audience (who thoroughly enjoy a good fight) into the mix and you have the formula for some meteoric rows. My parents are no exception.

Although my Father is, on the whole, an easygoing individual, if my Mother's actions meet with his disapproval he will let her know in no uncertain terms, whether they have the benefit of an audience or not.

One day, an ongoing argument results in my Mother (having ran up the stairs) being on the galleried landing of the hotel, where there is an enormous plant pot sitting on a large wooden chest. The pot, which is made of brass, is very big and very heavy. It is made still heavier by the soil and plant inside it. My Father is in the hall below. They are both shouting at one another. The argument is hoting up!

In order to reinforce her argument, my Mother, in the heat of the moment and despite her small stature, manages to lift the plant pot over the banister rail and lets it go. It makes the most incredible noise as it crashes onto the tiled floor beneath. It sounds like a bomb going off. The soil explodes out of it as if it were a bomb going off, though fortunately the shrapnel is harmless. Thankfully it misses my Father by inches, who, on seeing what is coming from above, is able to leap to safety – it is only his quick reaction that prevents a disaster. Had this heavy item hit my Father, it could quite easily have killed him.

Remarkably, the hall tiles and the marriage both survive; the pot does not. The impact crushes it into an unusable shape; it is given for scrap to aid the War Effort.

Realising how close that she came close to losing her husband because of this ill-thought-out act, my Mother is suitably penitent for a very long time to come.

24

The War Effort

The shortages of war result in a great deal of personal enterprise. A lady in the village starts to collect unwanted newspapers for the War Effort. She is often seen with a pile of newspapers on top of her Austin Seven that seem to defy gravity – the pile of papers being almost as high as the little car beneath.

Whenever she drives round the corner in front of the hotel, all of us watching are sure that this time the little car will turn over and it will be the death of her. However, it never does turn over and the papers are sold, and a great deal of money is generated.

Her endeavours are not wasted. Despite the fact that as the war progresses, newsprint becomes so scarce that the average paper is reduced to only four pages, she still manages to raise sufficient funds from her efforts to buy a mobile canteen to provide tea and coffee and meals for the troops. On one occasion it is based on the cricket ground at Dudley. Extra help is always needed and, although obliged to wear my old school overcoat, I happily take my place beside the WRVS ladies in their uniforms, making and serving refreshments. I am lucky enough on this occasion to be presented to the beautiful and elegant Princess Marina, a close member of the to Royal family. I am mesmerised by her flawless complexion, the first Royal skin that I have ever seen. She has come to inspect the troops and help keep up morale. She does a good job. We need to know that the Royals are on our side!

As for the newspaper collector, I do fear that in the end the newspapers may indeed have caused the demise of this lovely, kind and energetic lady. Rumour has it that she caught something nasty whilst handling the newspapers, which later results in her death.

Apart from the deprivations experienced by all, every household is expected to make its own contribution; the nation's pigs are short of food so large bins are distributed in streets throughout the country; newspaper advertisements chivvy us all with the request that fresh and dry food scraps be donated – the pigs of England must be fattened, it is for the good of the nation!

The call goes out for scrap metal and regular collections are made of anything that can be melted down to make aeroplanes or bombs. Most households volunteer metal pots, saucepans, old bikes, buckets and prams towards the War Effort. Our dented brass plant pot soon joins the collection. Meanwhile, the streets have changed dramatically as church gates and railings, and town and cottage garden fences are taken away for recycling.

Meanwhile, our individual efforts at enterprise are rather more self-centred. Unable to buy stockings, Gloria and I spend many happy hours staining ours legs brown with liquid leg makeup. The Government suggests using gravy browning for this job – we prefer to use the new cosmetics to do ours. We then take turns to draw 'seam' lines up the back of one another's legs using a black eye pencil. This is not an easy task and I doubt that anyone is convinced by the appearance of these wobbly 'seams'. Girls working in offices at this time are obliged to resort to old-fashioned lisle stockings if they cannot acquire nylon stockings, since to go to the office with bare legs is considered absolutely scandalous!

When lipstick is running low, and, not wishing to rely on the recommended alternative of beetroot juice to colour our lips, we find that it is possible to recreate a new one from the 'stubs' of several old ones. To do this we scrape the nub ends out of our used-up lipstick containers, putting the odd ends into an eggcup standing in a pan of water. This is then heated gently and the resulting liquid poured back into the container. Voila! A new lipstick! Not very good coverage, rather greasy if the truth be told, and sometimes a rather strange colour as the result of the mix of shades that go into the cup, but there is a war on and we must all do our bit!

Although unaware of it at the time, we later discover that the British obsession for wartime red lips (victory lips) and glamorous makeup could not have been a better reaction to the way Hitler wanted the women of his proud Arian race to appear. He detests anything that is not natural and insists that women wear no makeup, no lipstick and absolutely no nail varnish. They must not dye or perm their hair, wear high heels or diet to lose weight.

Well Herr Hitler, this is our way of demonstrating that your well-scrubbed Brunhilda-look is definitely not for us. And, as we are all working extremely hard on limited food rations, we have no need for diets!

25

Rationing

After the rationing of petrol, that of food and clothing follow shortly after. Soap, shampoo and stockings are hard to get. As well as both coupons and money being required to make food purchases, the Government also introduces a points system, which allows them to manipulate demand for various items, the 'point requirement' being directly linked to availability. When there is a glut of a particular product, the point requirement drops, and when there is a shortage the points increase. This is fair and works well for everyone. We are not subject at this stage to the deprivations caused by the ration book. This will come later. However, those less fortunate than us are allowed a weekly allowance of only one small piece of meat, 4oz of bacon or ham, 2oz of butter, 4oz of margarine or lard, 8oz of honey or jam, 8oz of sugar, 2oz of cheese, 2oz of tea, three pints of milk and some dried egg. Hardly a feast! Those able to eat in the school, office or factory canteen do so since it preserves the precious coupons.

Being situated in a rural location, there is no shortage of local vegetables, milk or eggs for us. The countryside has always been much more self-sufficient than the town, although by now many are Digging for Victory and suburban gardens have been turned into vegetable plots. Also, fortunately for us at the time, catering allowances are generous. We eat well and our customers do not need to use their coupons to purchase food from us. This fact annoys some, since those with the money to eat out are at an advantage over those without the money to do so. But the fact is that even during wartime those with enough money can buy pretty well whatever they want, within reason. A Black Market flourishes. Those in the know can purchase petrol, food and clothing coupons, or even the goods themselves. As ever, money talks. However, aware that many of her friends and customers are suffering because of the food shortages, my Mother, generous as ever, makes sure that as they leave at the end of the evening they take home a gift of butter, bacon, steak or eggs.

The meals most in demand in the restaurant are ham and egg, steak and chips and fish and chips. Despite the fact that fish is not on ration, many fish and chip shops have been obliged to use inferior fats to cook with, which result in an unpleasant-tasting end product. Those that are able to produce something nice inevitably have long queues. Our fish and chips taste good, sell well, and have the added benefit of no queue!

Our fish is always fresh thanks to its ingenious mode of transport. In order to get a twice-weekly delivery of very fresh fish to the hotel, a special arrangement has been made by my Father; an order is placed for a regular supply from the Birmingham Fish Market. Early in the morning it is wrapped in ice, boxed up, and delivered to the Midland Red Bus Station. From here it is put onto the Clent bus and driven the fifteen or so miles to the bus stop opposite the hotel. The driver then hops off the bus with this large, cold parcel, trots across the road and drops it onto the counter of the front bar. It is immediately transferred to the massive refrigerator that runs the entire length of the kitchen, from where it is ready to be cooked and served.

Meanwhile, alcohol is becoming much more difficult to get hold of.

Above: Pamela's father, Sid (the young boy on the right-hand side), joined the family business at an early age. This photograph shows his father's butcher shop on Ryland Street, Birmingham.(Author's collection)

Left: Sid as a teenager, just before he joined up. (Author's collection)

Above: Sid (top left) with his successful football team, Ladywood Wednesday, during the 1912/13 season. (Author's collection)

Left: Sid (centre) with his army pals, just after joining up in 1914. (Author's collection.)

With promotin, Sid gained Officer status and his life became very serious. (Author's collection)

Reflected footballing glory; as an Officer, Sid (pictured standing on the far left) could only watch his men play. (Author's collection)

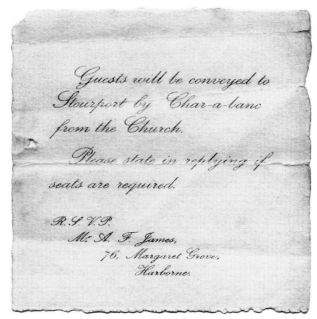

Guests will be conveyed to Stourport by Char-a-banc from the Church.

Please state in replying if seats are required.

R.S.V.P.
Mr A. F. James,
76, Margaret Grove,
Harborne.

Part of the wedding invitation to the marriage of Sid and Marie Wheeler, Pamela's parents. The ceremony took place at St John's Church, Harborne, on 10th of July 1922. (Author's collection)

Guests were conveyed to the wedding by charabanc. (Author's collection)

The happy couple and relatives. (Author's collection)

A serious and curly-haired
Pamela, aged four.
(Author's collection)

Pamela with the carer she
enjoyed biting. (Author's
collection)

The Woodman Hotel, Clent. (Author's collection)

Uncle Alf Joseph and Pamela. (Author's collection)

Four generations together. Clockwise from left: Grandmother Alice, Pamela, Marie and, seated, Gran-Gran at the rear of The Woodman Hotel in 1937. (Author's collection)

Pamela with her grandmother Alice in 1938. (Author's collection)

Pamela's first love, David, pictured in 1941. This photograph was given to Pamela as a keepsake following his tragic death. (Author's collection)

Pamela in 1941, aged seventeen. This picture was taken at the request for a photograph from some of Pamela's would-be suitors. (Author's collection)

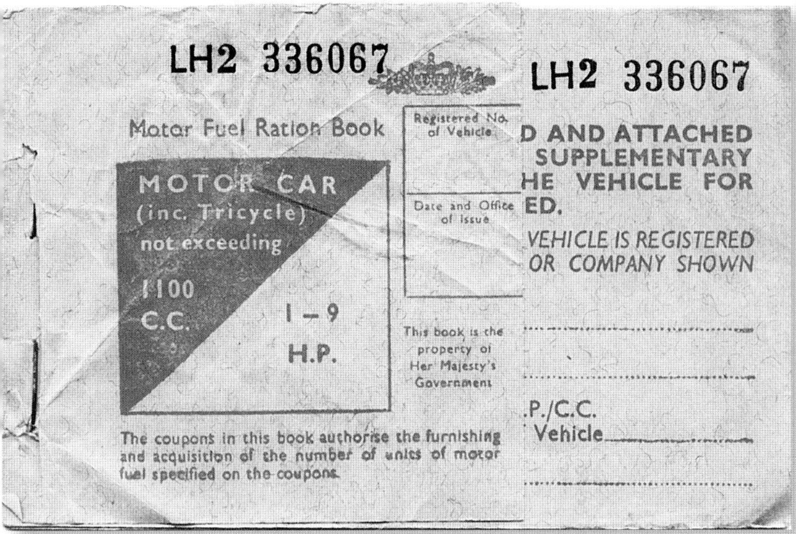

LH2 336067

Motor Fuel Ration Book

MOTOR CAR
(inc. Tricycle)
not exceeding
1100
C.C.
1 – 9
H.P.

Registered No. of Vehicle

Date and Office of Issue

This book is the property of Her Majesty's Government

The coupons in this book authorise the furnishing and acquisition of the number of units of motor fuel specified on the coupons.

LH2 336067

D AND ATTACHED
SUPPLEMENTARY
HE VEHICLE FOR
ED.

VEHICLE IS REGISTERED
OR COMPANY SHOWN

.P./C.C.
Vehicle

Petrol coupons were distributed during the war. (Author's collection)

John in his RAF uniform.
(Author's collection)

Pamela and John's official wedding photograph, 10th of November 1943.
(Author's collection)

Walter and Hilda Fellows, John's parents, at the wedding. (Author's collection)

Hilda and Marie (Pamela's mother-in-law and mother) at the wedding. (Author's collection)

Marie and her brother Fred at the wedding. (Author's collection)

Pamela (fourth from the right) was Maid of Honour at her friend Gloria's wedding at Pedmore Church in 1945. (Author's collection)

John's brother Rex, pictured around the time he joined up. He later won the Military Cross for bravery, aged just nineteen. (Author's collection)

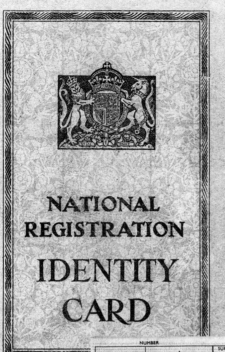

Pamela's Identity Card. (Author's collection)

Because of these supply shortages, I am sometimes obliged to enforce my own rationing system for spirits from behind my bar. It is left entirely to my discretion. Knowing that I have only one bottle of whisky to last the entire week, I am often obliged to deny this spirit to any but our most loyal and regular customers.

On one occasion, having denied the existence of any of the requested drink to fulfil an order, I am caught out by the mirrored décor of the bar.

I have gone round the corner where the precious whisky bottle is hidden in order to serve a tot to a regular customer; it is out of sight from all, or so I suppose.

The sharp-eyed customer, who has probably hung around to try and catch me out, is very annoyed at having been denied his requested drink. He can, by leaning over the bar and aided by the small terrazzo mirror tiles on the back and side of the bar, see straight round the corner! Thus he is able to see exactly what I am doing. I am found out and he loudly voices his disgust at this deception!

He is not best pleased at having been denied his favourite tipple, so in the circumstances, in order to keep the peace, I am forced to serve him his requested drink. I make sure that in future no one can see my hidden supply.

26

Our Friendly Local Policeman

Although we are situated up a lane in a rural part of the county, our location has one considerable disadvantage, in that we are situated directly opposite the police station. The licensing laws are very strict; the magistrates will not hesitate to remove your licence if you are found to be retailing alcohol outside the permitted hours, and that is the end of your livelihood, with no further chance of re-entering the trade again.

We do, however, have a slight edge over the long arm of the law.

From the elevated area of the bar where I work, I can see directly over the top sash window of the police station opposite.

When the Sergeant rises from his desk to his feet, I can clearly see the moment when he puts on his helmet. This is all the notice that we require. The cry goes up that he is on his way and as he leaves the station, strolls across the road and enters the lobby, we are able to call time, cover the beer pulls with towels, pull down the shutters on the bar and persuade any customers still drinking to finish up. It is a perfect arrangement as far as we are concerned.

This works well for months; is he aware that he is advertising his arrival in advance in order to help us out? Or does he think our nightly preparedness suspicious?

We are soon to find out.

One evening, to my horror, I find him standing on the left-hand side of my bar; I am still serving and it is well after time.

He has broken with his usual routine and entered the building through the rear entrance.

I am then subjected to a fierce and frightening dressing down. Such behaviour will not be tolerated again.

I have learned my lesson!

The policeman is a nuisance to our customers as much as to us, although to be fair, since there is a war on, he does have a job to do.

Those in power have decreed that no vehicle should be left overnight without the engine being disarmed; the rotor arm should be removed. The thought presumably being that an invading army might make use of this readily available transport for its own advantage. So one night (just after 11 o'clock) our friendly policeman has investigated the cars in the hotel car park to check how secure they are and has discovered that one has a near side door that is not locked. The engine rotor arm is still in place. Since almost any key will start almost any engine, this constitutes a serious offence. The fine can be £100! Our client, Mr Hood, is taken to court. Fortunately for our customer, the magistrates are of the opinion that the law regarding the disarming of car engines is not generally known at this early point in the war and so they are sympathetic. Mr Hood's fine is just £10.

We are to cross swords with this policeman again and next time it gets really nasty.

27

Cometh the Hour,
Cometh the Man

The war is now reaching terrifying levels. The news is bad. Battles are being lost. London endures continuous and unrelenting months of nightly bombing, designed to break the spirit of the population, though it does not. Hitler then turns his attention towards the provinces. When Coventry is blitzed on November the 14th 1940, we can see the glow of the fires from 40 miles away – the night sky is lit up; it is so bright we know that it must be very serious. The bombardment goes on for hours, as wave after wave of bombers attack. This beautiful medieval city is on fire; many thousands die in their burning homes. Although the intention is to force us into submission, the plan does not succeed, and, if anything, the shared misery serves to pull us closer together.

Hitler uses a German travel guide of England to pinpoint some of our most beautiful cities; he tries to break our spirit by destroying our most cherished architectural heritage as well as its unfortunate occupants. The lovely cities of Bath, Canterbury, York, Norwich and Exeter are amongst those whose cityscapes are altered in this way.

Families are divided when children are evacuated into the country to keep them away from harm, though many of these separations will go on to damage family relations in the future.

Many children die when a ship intended to deliver them to the safety of Canada is torpedoed by the Germans;

so many innocent young lives lost. As things progress and the news becomes more and more serious, I begin to wonder what will happen next. What is to become of us? Who can possibly help us to get through these terrible times? Apart from the guidance and kind words always on hand from my Father, there is another whose words always fill me with confidence, someone who makes me believe that we will defeat Hitler. A true leader, he helps to guide me and the rest of Britain through the darkest days of the war, at a time when it sometimes seems that all is lost.

That man is Winston Churchill, almost always seen with his trademark cigar in hand and his two-finger Victory sign; it is his speeches that keep us all going.

He has succeeded Chamberlain as Prime Minister. It was he who prediced Hitler's motives long before the outbreak of war; he who saw what was coming, proving those who thought him a warmonger wrong; he had been right all along

His oratory skills are legendary; he is always there with words of reassurance when we most need them. Whenever a speech is announced, the radiogram in the hotel is turned to full volume and a hushed silence falls over every room as we all listen with rapt attention to his words. He is an inspiration to us all.

Somehow, no matter how bad the news, we just know that when required we will expend the blood, toil, tears and sweat that he asks for.

We *will* fight them on the beaches and in the hills and we will NEVER SURRENDER.

And we never, ever do.

28

The Home Guard

Although deadly serious, the war is turning into a game of cat and mouse: the Government has ordered that all the signposts across the land be removed: we intend that the Germans will get hopelessly lost should they succeed with their invasion plans! The BBC stops broadcasting weather forecasts, since these might help the enemy; why should we aid them in this respect? The prediction of perfect, cloudless nights could prove too tempting for the enemy bombers. Hitler, in his turn, disguises train tunnel openings next to the river in Germany to look like castles, in the hope that they are assumed to be Rhine castles and thus far less likely to be subjected to bombing by the Allies.

With the German army advancing across Europe towards Britain, there is a genuine fear that invasion is imminent. Should the Germans invade, the South Coast of England is considered very vulnerable and since there are not enough fighting men available to keep watch, the roll falls to a group of volunteers. They will sound the alarm and then keep the enemy at bay, long enough for the trained and better-equipped professionals to come and deal with them.

It is not just the coastal areas that are of concern; among open areas of the country that are vulnerable, the Clent Hills and the vast wooded areas surrounding Hagley Park are also considered to be a prime target should the Germans invade.

Frequently over-flown by enemy planes, there is a genuine and well-placed fear that all of this open land will be a good place to parachute in under the cover of darkness. The surrounding woodland could easily hide an army!

However, with all but those in reserve occupations now called up, finding the men to form an army to protect the home front proves to be something of a challenge.

A group initially called the Local Defence Volunteers are rallied from the remaining population, those either too old or too young to go to war. Those unable to fight because they are occupied in jobs considered too important to leave (reserved occupations), are also able to help out in the evenings and at weekends.

What they lack in equipment they more than make up for with enthusiasm.

Because of his previous war experience, Father is very soon put in charge of our local group.

Our local battalion consists almost entirely of the young men from the village, those who at this point are too young to join up. Ours was more of a lads' army than a dads' army.

With no uniform for them to wear at this stage, they have to make do with Government-issue armbands sporting the initials LDV. When this name is frequently mocked as standing for Look, Duck & Vanish, the Government decides to rename them the Home Guard, for which new armbands are issued.

Our little Home Guard group is subjected to regular drill practice on the field behind the police station, the field where I once played cricket. I can hear my Father's commands of 'left, right, left, right about turn!' through the open windows of the hotel. He knows the value of discipline and soon knocks this little band of youths into shape. They realise that this is not a game and, despite their lack of years, they are aware of the gravity of the role that they may be expected to play. Father makes sure that they are well aware of what might lie ahead. They know that this is serious.

Father's command to 'present arms' creates something of a problem for his troop, because weapons are in very short supply. They are obliged to practice with anything that loosely resembles the proportion of a rifle; broom handles have to stand in for guns. However, plans are in place should things get really serious: should they be called upon to capture a German parachutist for example, shotguns and pistols (left over from the previous war) and even pitchforks will be made available and will be called into use. They take it in turns to practise how to use these weapons. An appeal made to the British public for supplies results in a huge number of weapons being handed over and America later sends rifles, but it is some years into the war before the Home Guard consider themselves properly equipped.

Despite the shortage of weapons and lack of proper uniform, our group takes their roll of protecting Clent and the surrounding area very seriously, and they frequently spend the night patrolling the hills in case the enemy attempts to parachute in.

On several occasions, Father sends Jack the barman up onto the hills with a crate of beer to help their night pass more pleasantly. After all, you have to keep the troops happy!

It is thanks to the vigilance of this group, who, having patrolled the hills for many evenings in the dark, are able to report back to my Father the actions of a young German maid working for an elderly lady living high up on the hill. Despite the strict rules of the blackout, she is seen opening and closing curtains as German planes are approaching. By giving these planes a fix on the ground, the young lady could be aiding the Germans to locate targets to bomb. She is challenged and told to stop, she claims ignorance, but when she is seen to repeat the action, she is arrested.

It is these young men, who, from the high vantage point on the hills, are able to spot the white-painted, flat roof of the big house below. Whether this is by accident or design is not clear, but this is not a time for taking chances and the appropriate action is taken.

This group of young men, as they attain the appropriate age, move on into the forces, but they have all served a useful apprenticeship, which will stand them in good stead for what lies ahead.

29

Party! Party!

Although tied to my job behind the cocktail bar, and the constraints laid down by my very strict Father, my social life is beginning to blossom.

By now, Gloria's father has established the family in a beautiful detached house in Pedmore and, since he loves champagne, music and parties, there is one held at the house every weekend without fail. He is a wonderful host and as he is one of my Father's best friends, he is completely trusted with my welfare.

So I am allowed – after the bar is shut, I have vacuumed the carpet and tidied up – to go and join the party. And since there are restrictions on travel, I am allowed to stay out for the night in the safety of Gloria's home. Her father (often still wearing pyjamas and dressing gown) never fails to deliver me back home on time, ready to start work the following morning.

The parties take place almost every Saturday night and I love the freedom!

Thanks to my wonderful dancing masters of the past ,and my illicit lessons, I know every step, so I am able to dance the night away.

My Father, although obviously aware that my social life starts rather late, assumes (wrongly) that after a couple of drinks I turn in, and, when I reappear in the morning back at home, I have had a good night's sleep. I am in no rush to disabuse him of this misapprehension.

There is a feeling of urgency amongst us all, the need to enjoy ourselves, to use every minute of life as if it is our last, rather like a condemned man. We are suddenly aware of just how short life can be. Why waste it sleeping?

So we actually do dance the entire night away, starting just before midnight and finishing as the sun comes up. Never have the words of the song 'Good Morning' been so appropriate; we have indeed 'danced the whole night through' and 'the milkman is on his way'. Often it is well after dawn when my head hits the pillow. It is very important that these late hours be kept from my Father. I know that he will not approve.

So on one occasion, after only two hours of sleep, I am back behind the cocktail bar, trying hard to smile but feeling pretty awful after so little sleep. Imagine my horror when a customer (a friend of Gloria's father who has attended the party of the night before) enlightens my Father as to the goings on of the previous evening.

'My goodness, your Pamela's got some stamina!'

'Oh really?' says Father.

'Don't know how the girl manages to do it! Just look at her, you can't imagine that she was still dancing at 4 o'clock this morning can you Sid?'

Oh dear, my cover is blown.

30

Gas Attack

From the moment that war is declared, Britain is on high alert for a gas attack. The Germans have used gas in the previous war and there is no reason to suppose that they will not do so again.

Everyone (men, women and children) has immediately been issued with a gasmask, supplied in a cardboard box with a strap made of string. It must be carried at all times. The strict rules mean that one is not allowed into the cinema without one; no gas mask means strictly no admittance!

The cinema has by now become an essential part of our wartime leisure activities. We need the light relief of the films on show, which have been carefully selected to lighten our mood. The emphasis on most of these movies is humorous escapism. A series of 'Road' films with Bob Hope and Bing Crosby are light and frothy entertainment. They make us forget our worries; we have a good laugh and we all leave the cinema with smiles on our faces, so much happier and more relaxed than when we went in.

From time to time we are all obliged to practise a rehearsal in case of a gas attack, at which point a wooden rattle is utilised, sounding (rather appropriately) like a poisonous and angry snake, to warn of an attack. The all clear is signalled by the sounding of a bell. Thankfully, as the predicted gas attacks never arrive, we have no need for long-term use of these disgusting, smelly things that make us feel sick when breathing through them, but we are obliged to have them with us for virtually the entire duration of the war. However, there is nothing to stop us introducing a little style into this obligatory piece of kit – not for Mother, Gloria and I a cardboard box on a piece of string! We are all in need of something far more stylish!

Being in business and a leading light in the local community, Gloria's father has contact with many interesting people and, as a result, can get his hands on most things, however scarce they may be. Amongst these contacts is a lady employed locally, working for a company that manufacture handbags for the Royal Family. From time to time she arrives at the hotel with a delicious collection at very low prices! This is how I acquire, amongst others, the most beautiful purple suede handbag, which is shaped to accommodate my obligatory gas mask in the base. The top is a handbag, silk-lined and large enough for a purse and lipstick. It is not my only gas mask bag but it is definitely my most stylish one.

We acquire silk stockings through a similar source but, sadly, realise that having been stored for far too long, they are 'shop rotten' and run into a mass of ladders the moment we try to put them on. Back to dying our legs with Silktona make up!

31

'Fronts'

We are all being encouraged to 'Make do and Mend', but wearing and rewearing the same outfits over months and years is a huge challenge for those interested in fashion. Clothing coupons are not generous. They do not satisfy anyone with a desire for a varied wardrobe of clothes. So my Mother, always bandbox smart, puts her sewing and designing skills to good use. Fabric is hard to find, though there are remnant sales and a limited amount of parachute silk is available. This silk has its shortcomings; all parachutes are cut on the cross and this makes using them to create any garment quite a challenge, since the bias creates a curve which proves very difficult to work with.

Nevertheless, she creates a pattern for a blouse; it is particularly ingenious since it requires the use of very little fabric.

She calls these garments 'fronts'.

This is a very apt name for, as you might imagine, that is all they are. No back! Just a front, held in place by the skilful use of ribbons.

By making a number of 'fronts' in a variety of different fabrics, she extends her wardrobe considerably.

They do, however, have one major shortcoming; in the event of hot weather, anyone succeeding in wrestling the jacket from her shoulders would have clearly revealed the major problem with the garment!

Despite my relatively young years, once out of school uniform I dress in smart two-piece suits very much like those of my Mother.

She and I both adore shoes; the love of which remains with me still. At this time though, leather shortages have started to impact on shoe designs, with flat shoes (which I dislike intensely) starting to appear in the shops. I *must* have heels and when cork-heeled wedges start to become fashionable, I am more than happy. Fortunately for me, these shoe fashions of the day are very forgiving for those whose job, like mine, entails spending many hours standing. Wedge-heeled shoes and sandals offer style and comfort for many hours' work behind the bar.

At this time I own the most wonderful pair of green snakeskin shoes, bought for me by Mother; they are my absolute favourites – very smart court shoes with very high heels – not suitable for work but perfect for special occasions. I am later to destroy these precious shoes when a date goes horribly wrong.

32

The Blackout

Two days after war is declared, the whole country is plunged into darkness. All street lights are extinguished, car headlights and reflectors are painted over and the local newspaper is full of prosecutions for those that do not comply. This unrelenting blackness, designed to save us from the bombers, causes much loss of life. People walk into unseen ponds, canals and ditches and drown. Drivers hit others cars, cyclists and darkly-clad pedestrians. One of our closest friends causes the death of someone when driving. He is not prosecuted.

The fact that everyone at this time is using coal to heat their homes adds to the problem, when thick smog (a side effect of burning coal and the resultant smoke belching from the chimneys) and prevailing weather conditions combines with the darkness of the blackout. This is particularly severe in the cities. Without any lights or landmarks, it is easy to get hopelessly lost. It causes chaos. Although carrots are recommended to improve our eyesight, sadly they do not have the power to make us see in the dark!

Light a match outdoors at the start of the war and, if spotted, you will be prosecuted, taken to court and fined 10 shillings. Later the fine for the same offence will be £1 10 shillings. Light two matches and the fine will be £2.

Chimney fires are also viewed as a potential aid to the enemy; fail to have the chimney swept and any ensuing fire will lead you straight to court and you will be prosecuted and fined.

Blackout curtains and blinds are obligatory, since even a chink of light can aid a foreign plane. Wardens are appointed to ensure that this rule is strictly adhered to and the cry of 'put that light out' is heard across the land. All lights must be switched off before outside doors are opened; absolutely no lights can be shown.

Naturally, the hotel car park lights are promptly extinguished and since we are in the depths of the countryside, if there is no moonlight, it is coal black.

So this is how I lose my beloved companion. My little dog Bonzo is run over on the car park and killed. It is ironic that one of the things he loved most in his life, the motorcar, is the means by which his life is brought to a premature end.

I cannot blame the driver of the car that hit him. The headlights that he is allowed to operate are useless, giving only a two-inch diameter hole of light, so dim that he can see nothing. In its way, it is an accident of war. Bonzo is buried in the garden. I have no idea where and no one tells me. For days they try to tell me that he has run away. I know that he has not!

I have lost my beloved and faithful friend Bonzo.

My lovely dog has gone and my heart is broken.

I have never felt pain like this before but I am soon to feel it again.

This is the first time in my life that I think my heart will break, but, sadly, it is not the last.

I am soon to suffer other terrible losses.

33

My Low-Flying Friends

Life expectancy in the services, particularly in the Air Force, is very poor. Only a quarter of bomber crews survive. Herr Hitler and his cronies reshape my future dreams several times as these lovely, handsome, brave young men who I am becoming so fond of – although not even having shared a kiss with – are first declared missing and then dead. It is unbearably sad.

Despite the shortage of petrol, many young (and handsome) servicemen do find their way to the hotel in between sorties. Some of them promise to overfly to say hello.

One Sunday morning the building starts to vibrate. All the dogs in the village are barking, everyone is out to see what the dreadful racket is about. A Stirling bomber is almost level with the chimneys; the noise is phenomenal. They are so low that I can see the faces of the pilot and crew quite clearly. I run outside on to the car park. They wave to me; I wave back. Unfortunately for them, my Father can also see who is perpetrating this foolhardy action and he is able to identify the main culprit, the pilot (Max), and demands (and later gets) an apology.

I get the blame. At a later date there was, by way of explanation, the suggestion that this low-flying exercise was in preparation for a raid to destroy a German dam but I don't think my Father is convinced.

Surrounded as I now am by so many dashing young men, my Father's rules become even more draconian.

I am not allowed to walk out of the hotel or onto the car park with any of them; under no circumstances am I to be alone with a young man.

However, I am aware that, among the group of boys who visit the hotel for a drink and a meal, I have a new admirer. He has been a regular visitor to my cocktail bar and has recently turned up in his Royal Air Force uniform, looking so very handsome. His name is David; I am smitten! And the feeling seems to be mutual. He invites me out and arrangements are made for us to attend a dance together when he is next home on leave, and since we know that my Father will not approve, we hatch a plan; we will tell him that I am going out with Gloria. No mention of dashing young RAF men at all!

One evening I prepare and serve a meal for him and his friends in the upstairs dining room. The meal is cleared away, the tables are pushed back, I am swept into his arms and we dance together. In this lovely, handsome, charming man I have found the person with whom I want to spend the rest of my life. No one else will do. He feels the same and says so. At the end of the oh so short evening, and, despite my Father's careful policing of my activities, I am able walk out on to the car park to wish him goodnight. He is twenty-four years of age and I am seventeen. It is a lovely late summer evening, and though it is not yet quite dark, there are small diamonds of stars shining above us. The faint sound of dance music floats across the still night air. While his friends wait in the car we kiss; just one kiss, but I adore him! I am head over heels in love. This is the boy that I will marry. We make a promise to take great care of ourselves and keep safe. I wave him goodbye, not knowing that circumstances are soon to prevent him from keeping his side of the bargain.

But this is wartime and life can be so very cruel.

On the following Sunday, I hear the noise of a plane flying overhead. I know at once that it is a Spitfire; its engine noise is unmistakable. Making considerably less noise than the bomber, this plane is much smaller and much higher in the sky. A single seater, the controls of this plane incorporate the gun trigger with which he will shoot down his enemy – a flying gun for the bravest of heroes! He flies high in the sky and loops the loop. I know at once who it is at the controls and that he is sending me a message. Following the incident with the Sterling bomber, I need to be more discreet in my acknowledgement of this visit, so I hightail it up to one of the upstairs windows and hang out, waving my tea towel by way of greeting: oh what excitement, my brave young hero!

How can I guess that I am never to see him again?

Days pass and I think of him constantly.

On Friday the 5th September 1941, I travel to Dudley to attend the wedding of friends. I am with Gloria. It is a lovely autumn day and a happy and joyful occasion. But partway through the service I am overwhelmed by the most awful feeling of doom. I am overcome with a foreboding so strong that it makes me feel ill. People around me enquire as to my wellbeing. I feel sick to the very core of my soul. I have never felt like this before in my entire life.

I tell Gloria that I am certain that my beloved boy has just died. But how can I possibly know?

But I do know. I am absolutely certain. And I am right.

Despite the reassurances from everyone at the wedding party that all will be well, when we arrive home later that day, confirmation of the dreadful news has arrived.

My premonition was correct.

Shortly after our precious evening together he is training in Scotland; he has had his wings (his pilot's licence) for just six weeks when his plane collides with another. Knowing that his disabled plane may crash onto nearby houses unless he stays at the controls, he does not attempt to save himself until it is too late. By the time he escapes, he is too near the ground, his parachute does not open fully, he does not survive. He dies a hero. When he is buried in Polmont in Scotland on the following Tuesday, a part of my heart goes with him.

I have the opportunity to attend his funeral to say my last sad farewell.

A close friend of David's will drive up to Scotland over the weekend; there will be enough room in the car for me.

Probably realising what a terrible ordeal attending this funeral will be for me, my Father finds a sound reason for me not to go.

My would-be chauffeur, already responsible for a serious accident that has injured a mutual friend, has developed a well-deserved reputation as an unreliable and dangerous driver.

Father decides that it is far too risky to let me travel such a long way with this young man.

One tragedy is more than enough to deal with.

So, numb with shock and grief, I concede that my final gift to David has to be delivered by proxy. I send him a wreath made up of twelve red roses, each one a symbol of my undying love. They are delivered to Scotland and placed on his coffin.

I write a poem on the reverse of his photograph: I have it still.

His laughing smile and carefree way will live in my heart until my dying day.

God bless you David.

I think my heart will break.

Shortly after this tragedy, Max also loses his life in his Sterling bomber when on a raid over Germany. He is among so many that we are never to see again. They are all so young, with their whole lives ahead of them.

We are told only the briefest of details (allegedly something to do with keeping the enemy in the dark, though in reality probably more to do with keeping up morale). Of the original group of twenty young men who come for a drink, the number diminishes week by week; they disappear one by one, never to be seen again. We know that they are missing or dead. We are not allowed to discuss it in any detail and this somehow makes it worse – it is horrible.

I find comfort at the time in the words of the song that Vera Lynn sings:

> We'll meet again,
> Don't know where,
> Don't know when,
> But I know we'll meet again some sunny day.

But this promise is never fulfilled.

We never do meet again.

They have gone forever.

What a dreadful, dreadful waste of life.

I can hardly bear it.

But what can any of us do but carry on? Hitler and the Third Reich must not defeat us; we must fight on until we win, so that is what we do.

34

The Card Game

The policeman from the station opposite has become a positive thorn in our side.

He has a job to do but we consider his interest in our business to be intrusive. One dark night, the Sergeant has decided to do a little detective work. He has crept in the darkness around the back of the pub and he is listening at a window. It is the window of the hotel kitchen.

It is after closing time and my Father is with three of his good friends (one of whom is the son of a local mayor, the other his brother; they are upstanding members of the community with reputations to protect). They are playing cards. Whilst it is permissible to play cards, to bet on the outcome is not. Gambling is strictly against the law.

The policeman listens to the conversation in the room and is convinced that a game of poker is in progress and that money is changing hands. He is sure that they are betting! This is illegal. He is pretty sure that he can hear drinks being sold after the permitted hours. This too is illegal.

This is serious and it is strictly against the law. They are charged. Much to my embarrassment, the story makes headline news in the local newspaper.

The ensuing court case requires the employment of the best legal mind that money can buy. There are reputations at stake.

My Father's livelihood is also at stake.

If the case is lost, so too is the hotel.

A leading QC is brought from London. His fees are enormous. But in law, as in the rest of life, you get what you pay for.

The Police Sergeant is adamant about what he heard that evening. He has accurate notes taken down at the window as the conversation was taking place – the whole thing is recorded in his notebook verbatim.

The word of a member of the police force – surely this cannot be argued with?

Well, yes it can!

Our shrewd and clever QC goes to the trouble of going back into the history of the weather conditions on the night in question. How much cloud? How much moonlight? We know for certain there will be no electric light around since the blackout is in full force. The blackout curtains guarantee that no light can escape from within. How, in the circumstances, is he able to see to write a single word? One of the card players is also able to point out that the hand that the policeman thinks he heard being discussed could not possibly be a hand in Poker!

And so we have him over a barrel!

It is proved, without doubt, that it was so dark, so pitch black, that it would have been absolutely impossible to make any sort of note in the prevailing conditions; you could not even see your hand in front of your face!

The case is thrown out.

We have won!

But is there a price to pay for this success; it is never a good idea to cross swords with the law. My Grandfather's prediction that this incident may have long-term consequences and might well backfire on my Father comes to pass.

A long time after the court case, the police arrive one evening and accuse my Father of stealing a car from outside a club. This ridiculous accusation, made all the more ludicrous given that he cannot drive, is based on evidence of 'a witness' who alleges that he was seen driving the car away.

This is a lie, but mud sticks and it takes many months for him to clear his name and to extricate any sort of apology from the police which, when it comes, is too late and very grudgingly given. It certainly looks to the cynical amongst us that they may have used this incident in an attempt to take their revenge.

35

The Date

Life still has to go on, and, with a fixed smile, I get on with doing what I have to do, despite my broken heart.

My parents can see this and encourage me to go out and enjoy myself.

Tom, a friend who is in the army, and in the summer had escaped from Dunkirk, is home on a fortnight's leave.

Dunkirk has been the most dismal failure for the British Army and their Allies; thousands have died in the fighting and the resulting situation could so easily have led to even more loss of life, a complete rout. The Germans have cornered the British on the beaches of North France. With the sea cutting them off to the front and the Germans closing in to the rear, their chances of escape are minimal. Churchill describes this event at the time as 'a colossal military mistake'. The men are sitting ducks for the Luftwaffe pilots to pick off at their leisure. The situation is considered so dire that prayers for salvation are offered up in cathedrals and churches throughout the land. And the prayers are answered. Tom's life, and those of many thousands of others, is saved by a selfless group of people who, despite the risk to their own lives, rescue the troops trapped on the beaches of France. Tom is picked up by one of the flotilla of small fishing and leisure boats – virtually anything that floats that rush across the Channel to help get our boys home. Later referred to as the 'Dunkirk spirit', this action by ordinary people in the face of adversity illustrated the pulling together of effort during that time, which helps us to win the war.

My Mother is very enthusiastic about Tom's offer to take me out; he is from a very wealthy family, but since their wealth has come as the result of embalming and burying dead people (they are undertakers), I am less than keen. He is a friend, but I do not see him as a future husband; for one thing, I do not relish discussing his day's work over dinner each evening!

However, my Father's permission is sought and given. So we set off to the cinema in Tom's yellow sports car. I am wearing my beautiful high-heeled, green snakeskin court shoes and, since I do not anticipate too much walking on this date, they are the perfect choice.

The film over, we adjourn to a pub. For some reason lunch gets overlooked. So, on an empty stomach, it does not require much alcohol to make me quite tipsy. Much later we arrive back in Clent.

On arriving home, and not wishing to advertise my condition to my Father (who is behind the bar), I attempt the stairs – I will go straight to bed, they need know nothing of my drunken state. Sadly, I do not make it. I fall noisily down the stairs from top to bottom, drawing a great deal of unwanted attention to myself. I am unharmed but the fall removes both heels from my beautiful shoes.

Both snapped clean off!

In my inebriated state, I am aware that my gait has somehow altered but I cannot work out why.

It transpires that I am now wearing is a pair of flat, green, snakeskin shoes – shoes that now sport a set of spikes where the heels once were!

Wondering what the noise is all about, I am now summoned into the bar by my Father. Unlike the hall, where I am able to tap easily across the tiles, the bar is thickly carpeted, so with each step my spiky-heeled shoes nail me firmly into the carpet. There is a risk that, unable to easily lift either foot, I am about to fall flat on my face. I am swaying but rooted to the spot by the nails where my heels once were.

'Pamela!' says Father sternly. 'Take off your shoes now and go to bed!'

I comply and, stepping out of my shoes, I abandon them where they are now fixed firmly to the carpet. It would not be wise in my condition to try to bend over to pick them up so I leave them where they are, nailed to the floor. In a vain attempt to regain what little dignity I have left, I wobble my way out of the bar and back across the hall. I attempt the stairs for a second time, now shoeless and clad only in stocking feet, and, happily, I am able to negotiate the stairs, this time without mishap, and go to bed.

The following day, Tom arrives to apologise to my Father. The apology accepted, he is permitted to take me to the Fountain Inn up the lane for a cup of coffee. Although this is when I am able to give him the photograph of myself that I have had taken at his request, I know at this time that he is not the man for me. He returns to his unit to carry on fighting.

I do not see Tom again until the war is over.

Meanwhile, my beautiful, green, snakeskin shoes are beyond repair.

36

Music, Music, Music

The radiogram in the bar has the facility to play five records at a time, which our customers are able to select themselves. There is also a repeat button, which allows one record to be played *ad infinitum*. One customer is particularly fond of a popular song of the day called 'The Umbrella Man', sung by Flanagan and Allen. It has a vaguely annoying refrain of 'toodle-luma-luma, toodle-luma-luma, toodle-oh-lay, any umbrellas, any umbrellas, any umbrellas to mend today'. Its refrain is one that somehow drills itself into your brain, allowing you to think of no other tune for days after. Whilst just about tolerable for two consecutive plays, it becomes deeply annoying after any more. My Father's patience, and that of the other customers, is pushed way beyond endurance levels, so at its fifth playing our customer is thrown out and told never to return.

The radio plays an enormous part in keeping our spirits high. Our local, medium-wave broadcasts are dropped for fear that the transmitters could aid the enemy with direction finding, and we now listen to the Home and Forces Service. As well as listening to Churchill's stirring speeches, which helps keep up our morale, we are also lectured by the Radio Doctor, Charles Hill, who advises us how to keep well during these difficult times. Radio programmes like *ITMA* (*It's That Man Again*), a comedy programme starring Tommy Handley with a series of rather inane catchphrases, which we all take up with great gusto ('Shall I do you now, Sir?'), never fails to make us smile. There is also *Hi Gang*, a comedy staring Ben Lyon and his wife Bebe Daniels. They bravely choose not to return to the safety of America but stay here in Britain, despite the risks, to make us laugh and keep up morale. There is *Music While You Work*, aimed at factory workers and usually broadcast onto the shop floor over the noise of the machinery. Despite the cacophony, all the workers join in with the singing. *Workers Playtime*, a touring variety show, is broadcast from factory to factory. There is a lot of laughter. We are in desperate need of music and humour, anything to lift the spirits; without it, the struggle, the shortages and the deprivations would have seemed impossible to bear.

War binds us all together in a way that absolutely nothing else could; we have a common enemy and it draws us closer as a community; it draws us closer as a nation. There really is such a thing as wartime spirit; complete strangers chat like old friends and offer lifts to people that they have never met before; the natural British reserve is lowered and people are happy to help one another. It helps all of us to get through.

37

The Abortion

One night my Mother's adored younger brother appears at the hotel. He is now a grown man and he accompanied by his girlfriend, but she is deathly pale and looks very unwell. He prevails upon my Mother to help them out. Since his young lady is clearly not well enough to travel home, could they please have a room for the night? Totally oblivious to the reason for this girl's illness, Mother ushers them into one of the hotel's guest bedrooms. It is not long before her condition worsens. What on earth is the matter with her?

Fred has to confess to my horrified Mother that she has just that day undergone the termination of an unwanted pregnancy. She has had an abortion.

At this time abortions are illegal. Backstreet abortionists often perform their gruesome task without anaesthetic, using unsterilized equipment such as knitting needles, and the consequential infections can and do lead to death.

But this frightened young lady was prepared to take the risk. The stigma attached to unmarried motherhood far outweighed any fear of the operation and its consequences. She would struggle to keep the pregnancy a secret. If the baby is allowed to enter the world, she would be forced to give it up to strangers. Her reputation would be gone. Abortion, despite all the risks, often seemed to be an infinitely better option than giving birth to an unwanted baby.

But now things are not looking good.

As frequently happens in these cases, she has started to haemorrhage, and since this huge blood loss is often the cause of death after such a procedure, my Mother knows that medical help must be summoned fast, or she could easily die. She does not hesitate to call the doctor, but in so doing she knows that attention – unwanted attention – is being drawn to the illegal actions of the pair. We could be in serious trouble by offering them refuge. This is a crime, which could land us in court. The doctor is called. The girl is treated.

The doctor points out to both my Mother and Father that, despite their ignorance of the events that have led to this situation, they are, nevertheless, implicated in the final consequences of a serious and illegal procedure, for which involvement the licence of the hotel could be forfeit.

We could lose our home and livelihood.

By rights he should inform the police.

By law he should inform the police.

But, as the local GP, he knows them both well. He knows that they would not knowingly countenance this action and he can see from the horror on their faces that they do not deserve to be punished for their entirely innocent involvement. He does not pursue the matter; he decides, on this occasion, that no useful purpose will be served and so he does not report the crime.

It is brushed under the carpet. The girl recovers. She and Fred leave. My Father is absolutely furious with Fred, whose name is now MUD!

Air-Raid Warnings

Directly opposite the hotel and adjacent to the police station there is a siren. It is stored in a lean-to building. The sound is one that I learn to fear and the noise it makes stays with me still. Starting as a slow whine, it builds to a high-pitched shriek that wraps cold hands of fear round my heart. The noise was terrifying.

The German bombers are now in the habit of dumping their unused and unwanted cargo on the Clent Hills, Hagley Park and the surrounding areas. They have flown over the factories and cities of the Midlands, doing their level best to destroy the aircraft and weapons factories, as well as the will of the populace, and have disposed of most of their deadly cargo. Now, however, getting rid of any remaining unused bombs becomes a matter of great importance. By jettisoning these bombs, their safe return to the motherland becomes more likely.

This act will lighten their load for a swift return home, allowing them to fly faster, to get higher than the searchlights and guns. Thus several bombs are dumped in this way very close to home, though fortunately none cause any damage.

Even before the horrible wail of the siren starts, we get a pre-air-raid warning. We know what is coming when all the lights in the hotel dip. It must be the demand that winding up the siren makes on the local electricity supply, but it is almost as scary as the noise of the siren itself. Stomach muscles tighten; here we go again, another night in the cellar.

The Searchlight Team

Around this time, a battalion of young soldiers is posted in a field about half a mile away from the hotel. They have responsibility for a searchlight. It is an important job because of the German bombers overflying the area. They are struggling with the cooking of their rations. With only basic equipment and probably no culinary skills at all, having just left home (where their mother would have been responsible for all the cooking), the food is proving to be pretty inedible. I am not quite sure how, but the fact that these gallant young men are suffering for want of a good meal becomes known to my Mother. She has the solution. If they deliver the food (which is usually a joint of meat) to the hotel kitchen, she will prepare and cook it for them and they can then present themselves at the appropriate hour to eat it.

It is her contribution to the War Effort.

Leaving the searchlight behind they set off, marching in single file across the field. They arrive at the hotel, are seated round a large table and thus the delicious meal is consumed. As one might anticipate, a certain amount of beverage is consumed also. Well, what would anyone expect a soldier to do when marched to a place licensed to sell intoxicating liquor?

The whole thing is considered by all to be a huge success. My Mother has helped the War Effort, my Father is probably quite happy to have sold some beer at a time when customers were becoming increasingly rare, and the soldiers are now mellow, the prospect of another night under canvas seeming much more attractive from the other side of several pints of beer. Everyone involved is keen to repeat the exercise. It is true to say, however, that the march back across the field to the searchlight was not as rigid a formation as that on their arrival.

Well, as the saying goes, 'much wants more', and by the time several meals have been marched to and enjoyed, the march home has turned into a drunken shambles. One of the men, the sergeant in charge, had consumed so much beer that he had to be carried back across the fields. Sadly for him, his senior officers had chosen that night to do a spot-check. He was stripped of his stripes! It is at this point that the Company Commander became aware of the goings on. We receive a visit, when he points out to my Mother that a drunken searchlight team will not assist the War Effort in any way and that from now on we are out of bounds to his men!

We do not see the searchlight team again.

Among the young men who visit the hotel around this time is a young man called John Fellows, known to most of his friends as Jack, and although I am unaware of it at the time, this is the man with whom I am destined to spend most of the rest of my life, the man that I will marry and with whom I will have two children. At this stage he is engaged to another – she is in the ATS (the Auxiliary Territorial Service). These women are not expected to fight but are part of the larger War Effort at home, filling all sorts of roles left vacant by the men who have been called up. John has not yet joined up but is gainfully employed in the making of aeroplanes at a local factory.

Even though I barely know him, have rarely spoken to him and have not recovered from the loss of my beloved David, he immediately decides that I am 'The One'. He breaks off his engagement and starts to pursue me.

40

Refugees

By now, the nightly bombings in Birmingham and its suburbs have reached terrifying proportions. With its many factories manufacturing aeroplanes, bombs and guns, it is now the third most bombed city in Britain – only London and Hull suffer more, though surely this is a competition that none of us wants to win. We do not know these alarming facts at the time, however, since the radio broadcasts allude only vaguely to 'an air raid in a Midlands town last night', the plan being that we, the general public, and the enemy are kept in the dark.

It is the broadcasts from Radio Hamburg in Germany of William Joyce – known as Lord Haw Haw – that we try hard NEVER to listen to. For he is able to provide considerably more information than our own Government is prepared to share with us, which somehow makes it even more frightening. This Irish man broadcasting from Germany mocks us via the airwaves; he seems to know so much more about the progress of the war than we do! He derides our leaders and questions our victories. His loyalty to Hitler and the Third Reich is rewarded shortly after the war ends – with his execution.

By now, those who can no longer bear the nightly ordeal of bombing, if in possession of a car and sufficient fuel, are leaving the city with blankets and thermos flasks to sleep in their cars in the country lanes. It seems a safer option. And it is probably no more uncomfortable than spending the night in a spider-filled Anderson shelter in the garden. These corrugated-iron shelters are a refuge supplied in kit form to all households by the Government, but they are not renowned for offering any degree of comfort to its occupants. With the area above ground covered in soil, they offer those within, a degree of protection from the shrapnel falling nearby, but will not survive a direct hit. Buried four feet underground (with two feet above), they are damp, noisy and cold. Despite the fitting of sumps for drainage, they often part fill with water, so are far from comfortable but since few houses offer the relative safety of a cellar, they are, at this stage, often the only alternative to the cupboard under the stairs or, for the lucky few, an escape by car to the country. Later in the war, in order to assist those citizens without gardens, the Home Secretary introduces the Morrison shelter; it is to be used indoors and consists of a metal cage with a solid steel top. This is designed to protect those inside from falling masonry. The space inside is just about big enough for an adult couple to lie side-by-side, providing that neither is claustrophobic.

At this point my Mother decides that, providing that there are no objections from them having to sleep on the carpeted floor, these temporary refugees who have driven out from the city can spend the night in the hotel bar. For this there is no charge. We heat milk up for the babies and provide free tea and coffee for the adults. Mother does, however, take the opportunity to sell a ham and egg breakfast to those who want it before they set off back to their jobs in the city in the morning. Little do we realise that we are soon to join the ranks of these refugees.

The fight to keep the hotel viable and afloat has failed.

From the onset of the war and with the subsequent shortages created by fuel rationing, the effects on the business have started to bite. Although gradual at first, they get progressively worse.

The moment that the war begins, petrol rationing is introduced, and these shortages impact on our customers both old and new. In the early months, people trying to maintain a sense of normality manage to eke out their allowances. It is possible to turn off the car engine at the top of a hill and coast for long distances, a little trick that will save fuel. But as the war progresses, under no circumstances can precious petrol be wasted on anything as frivolous as a drive out into the countryside for a leisurely drink, and anyone caught doing so could be in severe trouble. Even jail sentences can be expected for those found breaking the rules. Most people comply without question; cars are locked away until the war is over. Our more famous residents have to find hotels close to the theatres in which they perform.

So, being situated well out in the countryside, at least two miles from the nearest village (which in any event boast their own hostelries to which the locals can walk), and three or four miles from the nearest market town, the footfall drops dramatically.

Only the most energetic would attempt to walk or cycle here, and the nightly blackout represents a very real risk to anyone venturing out after dark of being run over by one of the few vehicles still on the road.

The situation is not helped by the arctic weather conditions of 1940. It is absolutely bitterly cold. The Thames freezes over for the first time in centuries. We suffer from ice storms that freeze on contact with the ground, turning pavements into lethal skating rinks. When snow falls on top of the ice it becomes even more dangerous. Deliveries cannot be made since conditions make most roads impassable.

The weight of the ice brings down telephone and power lines. Incendiary fires become difficult to put out as fire-fighters struggle when the water in their hoses freezes.

Spring seems such a very long way off.

Almost unbelievably, the winters of 1941 and 1942 throw equally bitter weather at us, as if we don't have enough to cope with!

By 1942 there is no petrol available at all for the use of the general populace. Only emergency and public vehicles, and those involved in the war, can be seen on the road.

Many years ago (probably around the time that the hotel was built and quite possibly the reason for its creation) there had been plans to bring a rail line through to Clent, very close to the Woodman. What a difference its existence could have made to our fortunes now. At this time the trains are the one form of transport that does not suffer any cuts; they operate night and day taking troops across the country. But, sadly, there is no rail line and hence no trains, which might have helped our business survive.

There are few buses to catch other than those taking people to and from work, and in the evening all the schedules have been dramatically curtailed in order to save petrol.

There is absolutely no passing trade.

This has always been a property location that relies almost entirely on the motorcar for its trade.

No petrol.

No cars.

No customers.

No business.

The hotel is a large building, expensive to heat and light. Overheads are huge. The rent, though easy to cover in good times, seems an impossible burden in bad times. All of the original staff of fourteen have by now been called up and are fighting for King and Country. Only Jack the barman, Mother, Father and myself have stayed here to keep the place going, and we have had to work very hard to do so. With fewer and fewer customers and large overheads, the financial sums just do not add up.

Although Father manages to keep the true situation of our finances secret for some months, he eventually concedes defeat and relinquishes the tenancy back to the brewery.

We have to leave.

Father has yet another reason to hate the Germans.

The war has ruined us.

41

The Air Raid

So The Woodman Hotel, where I have spent my adolescent years, is now left behind and we move on. Suitcases are piled into the car and off we go. Father has managed to secure the lease on a top-floor mansion flat about half a mile from Birmingham city centre. One somehow cannot imagine that there was much competition for this property, particularly in view of the bombing that has been increasing nightly, but as the saying goes, 'any port in a storm'. We are leaving the relative safety of the countryside. We are entering dangerous territory.

And my first air raid experience is very nearly my last.

When we arrive at our new home I am impressed. The apartment is elegant and spacious with high ceilings and cornicing. We are on the top floor; the views overlook Islington Row and much of the city. All the furniture, fixtures and fittings of our previous life have been left behind, sold to the new tenant of the hotel (and the very best of luck to him!). Our new home, despite the shortages of war, has been newly furnished, and, with the taste of my ever-stylish Mother, it looks lovely. But on the way here we have passed many bombed-out buildings, so how do we know that we won't be next?

John has come calling.

He has borrowed his brother Rex's motorbike (without asking), his determination to make me his girl not daunted in the least by the risk of bombs.

The Germans come calling shortly after.

I am very frightened. The slow wail of the air-raid siren is rising and the search for the key to the shelter is in full cry. There is one large air-raid shelter for all the residents of the block, there is only one key, and there is one caretaker who looks after it.

And he is nowhere to be found.

The shelter is locked.

The caretaker is in hospital.

He is suffering from incendiary bomb burns.

The key is in his pocket.

The air-raid shelter is inaccessible.

And then the bombing starts.

Unable to get into the shelter, the residents of the flats are all gathered on the ground floor of the block.

'On the floor,' commands my Father, 'hands over your ears!' His years as an Officer are not forgotten.

We all comply without question. The action saves our lives. When it is over we inspect the shrapnel holes. Most are at waist or head height – anyone standing would have been hit.

Meanwhile, the shelter to which we have all been denied access, has received a direct hit.

No one in the shelter would have survived.

Unable to return to our flat, we are forced to spend the remainder of the night on the ground floor of the block. Sitting on the concrete floor and in severe discomfort, we are unable to sleep; shock and adrenalin levels do not permit.

John sees this as a good time to propose marriage. I decline; I feel that I barely know him, but we have survived this terrible ordeal together.

Early the next morning, his brother Rex, furious with John for taking his transport without asking and desperate to locate his missing motorbike, arrives to claim back his property. John's plan to return it the previous evening before it was missed was not possible, having been thwarted by the German bombs.

Outside the scene is surreal; the lampposts are hung with items of clothing, the shop windows have gone, there is broken glass everywhere. The local furriers are quick to board up their windows; the fur coats inside would be of great value to anyone considering looting.

John and Father go up to the flat to inspect the damage. They are able to get access to the top floor only with extreme caution. The lift is unusable so they are obliged to wade up the stairwell, through shards of broken glass from the blown-out windows. Mother and I remain in the relative safety of the ground floor.

When they return the news is not good.

Our lovely new home is wrecked. Every window has gone and the curtains are in tatters; they have torn themselves to shreds, flapping in the wind against the broken glass. The cabinet that held my Mother's collection of china and glass lies on its side, its contents smashed to smithereens. Everything is wrecked. There is hardly anything salvageable.

The blast which destroyed the air-raid shelter has blown a sizable hole in the side of the block and part of the roof has gone. It is no longer fit for habitation.

We manage to rescue only the suitcases that we had not even had time to unpack. My worldly goods are reduced to just a few clothes, a pair of shoes, a few books and some letters. We own little more than we stand up in. We have been bombed out. We too are now refugees.

I start to shake.

I shake for a very long time.

42

Family War Efforts

Although John is not yet in the services, occupied as he is with the construction of aeroplanes, he does have ambitions to fly. One way and another many members of the family are making a contribution to the War Effort.

His own father, an accountant at a local steel works Stuarts and Lloyds is, unbeknown to us, becoming involved in an ambitious project, which will have a profound and important effect on the final outcome of the war. He sometimes travels to the coast on a mysterious mission, about which he enlightens no one. He is preparing the costing for a project called PLUTO (this mnemonic stands for Pipe Line Under The Ocean). Problem? How do you fuel the vehicles of war whilst in a foreign country? (A very serious problem in wartime.) PLUTO is to provide the ingenious solution!

The imaginative scheme created by Lord Mountbatten involves the manufacture of lengths of steel pipe, which will reel off the back of a ship. This pipe will then sink to the sea bottom. It will then be used to supply fuel from England to France. The pumping stations on the British coast and on the Isle of Wight are cleverly disguised to match the surrounding buildings. This project, according to Churchill, plays a critical part in the winning of the war and, without it, we would almost certainly not have succeeded. We knew nothing of it at the time. It was absolutely TOP SECRET. We learn later that the pipeline is so successful that it is reeled out across Europe as far as Berlin, fuelling the lorries and tanks of the victorious forces.

As John's kid brother Rex is later to show, he is made of stern stuff! His bravery will be demonstrated when, at only nineteen years of age, he leads his men to capture a German bunker with no regard for his own safety. Mentioned in Dispatches, he will soon have medals to prove it.

John's cousin Derek will go on to rescue a number of injured comrades from minefields, receiving medals for his bravery. Whilst performing these tasks, he will suffer a permanent disability as the result of explosions.

Although he enjoys building planes, he would much rather be flying them.

So John enlists.

His RAF training has started in Scotland.

We, meanwhile, are homeless!

Remarkably, following the bombing and despite being parked close to the flat, Mother's little car has survived. So we are able to pile our last few possessions in and seek refuge for a few nights.

In times of adversity it is said that you find out who your friends are. We found ours! Bombed out of a home that we had barely spent a night in, we are taken in by friends of my parents called Jim and Renee Parkes. They have a café in Quinton and manage to shoehorn us into the tiny accommodation above their café. We are able to camp out with them for a few weeks.

As well as being an inventor and entrepreneur, the rather eccentric Jim (who is rumoured to use a shotgun to clean his chimney) has a very pragmatic approach to the shortages of war.

Unable to get petrol for his business and leisure activities, he acquires a pony and trap to carry him and Renee to the pub and the shops.

On one occasion, they have visited a pub about a mile from home. They have enjoyed a pleasant time, but it is late and as the evening is coming to an end, Jim has had enough and wants to leave. His wife, meanwhile, does not.

'I am going now,' says Jim.

'Well I am not. I want another drink. Don't you dare take that trap without me in it!' hollers Renee.

Shortly afterwards, the sound of hooves are heard on the tarmac road outside. When we all go out to see what has happened, we find the trap and the traces propped up against the wall of the pub – Jim has done exactly as he was told, he has detached the pony from the traces of the trap, left it for his wife as requested, and ridden the pony home bareback!

Renee is forced to walk the mile back home.

I do not recollect the ensuing argument but it is not long before we move on and their hospitality is replaced by that of the Josephs (he of the water otter). We spend several weeks with them in Hagley, where we are looked after as cherished guests.

It is around this time that Mother is forced to part with her car. As there is no longer any petrol available, there is absolutely no point in us keeping it.

My Father, meanwhile, is struggling to find somewhere more permanent for us to live.

43

Call-Up

Although housing is now very difficult to find, my Father has managed to secure another roof over our heads; this time we move to Halesowen. This is important, as I have now been called up to a factory job in Birmingham.

For this job I wear thick trousers and as many layers of clothing as I can manage. It is absolutely bitterly cold. A knotted headscarf keeps my hair out of the way of the machinery; this is a sensible precaution, girls have been scalped for not complying with this rule.

The factory job is dirty, smelly and dangerous. I am doing a man's job in an otherwise exclusively male unit making parts for aeroplanes. My predecessor has been called into the army and I replace him, producing the same output in the same timescale, but there is no piecework here. I am paid only a woman's rate for the job. There are other females working at the factory in an inspection unit, but for some reason I am thrown in with the men and they are not in the least bit welcoming. The swarf drilled from the components is hot and gets in my eyes and burns me. I am sometimes taken to hospital to have treatment for these burns. The men resent my presence. I resent the fact that I am not getting paid the correct rate for the job. I become rather militant. There is talk of union involvement. I am all for it.

One morning I arrive early for work and discover a dead rat on my chair, clearly a gift from my male colleagues, and since I am terrified of even the smallest mouse, this is a test of both my resolve and my acting skills. I will NOT let them see what I really feel. 'I consider you lot to be rats and if you don't remove this creature immediately, I am going straight to the bosses and I will report the lot of you!' My bravado pays off and the creature is removed.

It is during this horrid time in my life that John returns from Scotland with the news that he is about to be posted to Canada for further training. His ambition to fly is getting closer.

He has been very determined and dedicated in his suit.

And after all, we have survived a near-death experience together.

'Now will you marry me?'

'Well, yes, I will.'

44

The Wedding

Because of John's posting to Canada, the marriage needs to be organised at very short notice, which requires a special licence. In order to wed in the pretty church of St Kenelm's at Romsley, and being resident in Halesowen (outside the church's official catchment area), a small amount of deception is called for.

To marry in this beautiful little country church, one should really live in the village. However, there is a way round this rule provided that you know the right people. In order to qualify for this residency, all that is necessary is to deliver a suitcase full of clothes to a willing local resident whose home lies within the required area and is prepared to take part in this innocent deception. Thankfully, the mother of a friend who lives in a nearby cottage is happy to oblige. The suitcase is delivered, the special licence acquired, I am to marry!

Putting together a wedding outfit is a challenge. No white dress for me (though I more than qualify to wear white under the usual terms and conditions of the day). Time does not permit. Coupons are collected together and Mother and I venture into Birmingham city centre. I choose a pale blue woollen Berketex suit (it is to be a November wedding). I wear a tan hat and tan shoes. John will look fetching and very handsome in his RAF uniform. I do not carry a bouquet but I have a corsage of pink roses on my lapel.

My silk stockings have been hoarded for some months, but on the day of my wedding I find their major shortcoming is the fit; they are at least a size smaller than my long legs really require. There is every chance that when I kneel at the altar they will not cope with the strain! Not relishing the prospect of walking back down the aisle with my stockings a mass of ladders, I decide that the solution is to use only the front suspenders to keep them in place; not ideal, but only I am aware of this discomfort.

On the morning of my wedding – November the 10th 1943 – Fred arrives at the house. My Mother greets her little brother with great joy – she is looking forward to a day of celebration and after so much sadness and upheaval who can blame her? So the champagne is cracked open early. My Father, not having forgotten nor forgiven the events of the past (and never likely to), goes out into the garden and stays there. He refuses to be under the same roof as him. Fred and Mother continue to celebrate my nuptials with alcohol. Any excuse for a party!

My Mother likes my husband-to-be a lot. He is good company; they both love parties and he has proved an enthusiastic drinking companion for her. My Father is less keen on my forthcoming union.

And so, later, on this crisp November morning when I find myself being driven up the lanes to St Kenelm's Church, he is advising me quite vehemently (and much to the bemusement of the taxi driver) that I can, at any time, issue the instruction for the vehicle to be turned round to take us both home; he is clearly not keen to lose his precious daughter!

I do not take his advice. I am happy to make my vows and not much more than half an hour later I find myself a married woman. I am now Mrs Pamela Edith Fellows.

Unfortunately, my Mother's earlier encounter with the champagne has left her a little the worse for wear, which results in her signing the church register in her maiden name; a fact that (much to my huge embarrassment) she shares loudly with the rest of the congregation and guests in the church. This information prefixed, given the location, with the singularly inappropriate oath of 'JESUS CHRIST!'

The service over, John and I take the taxi back to a photographer's studio in Halesowen. Although a friend has managed to take a few informal snaps at the wedding, in the absence of an official wedding photographer, this is our only option to record the occasion for posterity.

Since there is no colour film available, we opt to have the resulting photographs hand-coloured. Sadly, when I collect these photos at a later date I am horrified at the result. Our faces and hands are coloured to match the pink roses of my corsage. We look ridiculous! Never has the phrase 'blushing bride' been so appropriate; we are both the colour of cooked prawns! Despite the protestations of the photographer, who tries to assure me that they will fade in time, I insist that they are redone in black and white.

Meanwhile, the rest of the guests adjourn to the Lyttleton Arms in Hagley for the wedding breakfast. We join them later. It is quite a modest affair with just a few friends and family and when it is over, we wave goodbye to our guests and, thanks to a mix up with the taxis, which have all been sent away by error, we are obliged to walk the two miles to the railway station in Stourbridge. From there, we travel by train to Worcester for our all-too-brief honeymoon. Two nights only and then back to my parents' home. John then returns to Scotland, from where we are expecting that he will travel on to Canada to continue with his training.

What we do not know at the time is that he is about to receive a crushing rejection; his cherished hopes of becoming a pilot are soon to be dashed.

For it is around this time that an eye test reveals John's colour blindness; his inability to differentiate between green and blue (land or sea) could prove lethal to a pilot and his crew.

His dream of flying is shattered.

Knowing how dangerous this career choice is proving to be for so many young men, we really should be relieved at the news. He is not. He was looking forward to the daredevil life at the controls of a Spitfire. He never gets to Canada. He is posted first to Anglesea and then onto Aden, where he remains until well after the war is over.

Sand instead of snow.

My factory job is terminated. Now that I am a married woman, they suggest that my working hours are not going to be compatible with the domestic requirements that my new role as wife will demand of me!

Also, I am an increasingly militant thorn in their side. They are as glad to see the back of me as I am of them. I am more than happy to be leaving. I hate this job and the arrangement is convenient for both sides.

The Land Army

While employed at the factory, I save all the money that I earn towards the home that I dream of setting up when my husband comes home for good.

He is allowed home on leave but I see him rarely, so our snatched moments are precious. Here I am, a married woman, still living at home with both parents and saving every penny that I can get. I am not to know it at the time, but all of my precious savings are to be blown on a car when John returns from war. Not the plan that I had in mind.

But not knowing of its future use, I concentrate on the need to keep my little nest egg growing; I need to find another job.

Miracle of miracles, I am interviewed for a job with the Land Army. I take the bus from Halesowen and walk up the long drive to the farm. It is situated in the little village of Broome near Clent. I am almost back to my roots, for had we not left the hotel, it would not have been much more than five minutes from home.

I arrive for the interview and am invited into the large kitchen of the farmhouse and sit down. I am wearing a smart suit and high court shoes, as if applying for a job in an office. Mr Pheysey, the farmer, looks me up and down and probably thinks this overdressed townie may not be up to the challenge.

The work will be hard, physical and tiring.

'Have you got any flat, brogue shoes?' he asks. 'You can't wear shoes like that to work on the land dear.'

Well as it happens, no, I don't have any, but I can get some I am sure. And, of course, my ever-resourceful Father provides the requisite footwear and I am ready to start on the following Monday. I have on my flat, brogue shoes, my dungarees and a cotton shirt; the outfit is in its own way quite fetching. We all wear headscarves to keep our hair out of our eyes and the corn out of our hair.

The Land Army is a group of women drafted in to replace the men who have been called up to fight. We wear khaki dungarees, use an outside privy and wash in a cold-water pump in the yard. The only men left on this farm are those too old to be called up and the farmer himself. But they are able to pass on their years of experience and they teach us all that we need to know.

There are two working horses to pull tractors and carts, so no need for petrol-consuming machinery here.

We work long hours in all weather. We plant, we hoe and we harvest, and I love it! On my first day I am so famished that I have eaten my sandwich lunch by 11 o'clock: a mistake that I do not repeat again.

I need to start early; too early for the buses from Halesowen, as the timetables have been dramatically curtailed by the petrol shortages of war, so I go on my bicycle.

It is a lovely ride out. Fairly flat for a couple of miles and then a long coast down a big hill, hardly any pedalling at all and lots of fresh air – this is so much nicer than the dirty factory!

Sadly, this same hill has to be tackled on the return journey and it proves a mighty challenge. Already exhausted from a day's hard labour, it looks almost insurmountable.

On one of my first days a kind lorry driver stops and suggests I throw the bike on the back and jump in.

'Certainly not,' I say. 'I have been told never to accept a lift from strangers.'

'Please your bloody self,' he says and drives off.

How often I think of that kind driver as I slog up the hill in the coming months, but I receive no further offers of a lift, though, by now, I would jump at the chance.

By the end of that summer I am tanned, supple, fit as a fiddle and expecting my first baby.

When my advancing pregnancy forces my retirement from the Land Army, my sister-in-law, Megan, takes over my job on the farm.

Meanwhile, the war in Europe has been progressing. The month that my pregnancy is confirmed – August 1944 – there is good news from Italy; first the Allies take Florence; Pisa follows shortly after.

The Italians have developed a reputation for not liking fighting very much and, sensibly, they are happy to hand over their weapons and go home. And who can blame them? We are all sick to death of war.

But despite losing their Italian Allies, the Germans are fighting on and the bombardment of Britain continues at a pace; they are not giving up that easily. A new and terrifying range of self-propelled weapons has been developed; the V1 and V2 rocket bombs, unmanned and indiscriminate, are being launched from the French coast and are delivering death and destruction on a grand scale to the south of England.

But whatever is happening on the French and English coasts, in the heartlands of Europe huge progress is being made on the ground and little by little the news is improving; we have Hitler on the back foot, and now my confinement chimes with many significant dates in the war.

By January 1945 most of the enemy are on the run, major cities fall to the Allies like a tumbling house of cards. Maybe we can win this war after all?

★

I, meanwhile, busy myself gathering the things necessary for a new baby. The Government provides copious amounts of orange juice and ghastly cod liver oil for me to drink, to ensure that the next generation has the benefit of strong bones and teeth. Due to my condition, I have now been issued with a different coloured ration book, green instead off beige. This entitles me to a full pint of milk, the first choice of fruit and a double ration of eggs. My doctor suggests stout as a good way to keep my iron levels up. So I drink half a pint of Guinness daily. Maternity wear is limited but I am able to buy wrap around tops designed to accommodate my increasing girth. By good fortune my best winter coat is a swagger cut, perfectly designed for a mother-to-be!

I acquire a hand-me-down cot from the family, together with bedding, and I am lucky enough to be able to purchase a new pram. Much knitting is done; matinee jackets, hats, bonnets, bootees and mittens being the order of the day, whatever the season. Everyone rallies round to provide the necessary requisites for the expected baby.

A bed is booked for the birth in a local nursing home, where I am successfully delivered of a beautiful baby girl; she is born on April the 10th. John does not attend the birth, as is the practise of the day, but he is allowed a weeks' leave to see us both. We have no home of our own, few possessions, and I am still living with my parents. But we have hope that it is nearing an end.

We find out later that only twenty days after the birth, on April the 30th, our archenemy, the detested Fuehrer, takes his own life.

Around this time, we hear the most horrifying stories coming out of Germany. Richard Dimbleby, a BBC reporter, is broadcasting live from a concentration camp called Bergen Belsen. He tells of thousands of people, many of whom are Jewish, who have been kept in the most inhumane conditions. Here the veneer of civilisation has completely disappeared. Men, women and children have been shipped in by the trainload, from all over Europe, their possessions stolen and then they have been systematically murdered by the Nazis. Gassed, or starved to death. Bodies lie unburied, survivors are walking skeletons, barely recognisable as human beings. We learn later that this was to be Hitler's 'Final Solution'. This is how he will remove from the face of the earth anyone that he feels does not deserve to live, those who do not fit his idea of Arian perfection.

Someone we know quite well is also there not long after the liberation of this camp. He does not say much about what he has witnessed; it is a memory too awful to share, but he tells us that the advancing army were aware of the stench of death hanging over the camp from many miles away.

Later, film footage emerges showing the dreadful conditions inflicted on these poor people, but only for those with a strong enough stomach to watch. Around the same time, the German people are herded into cinemas and forced to witness what their wonderful leader and his henchmen were really up to!

This has been a very close call! This could so easily have gone the other way. Whatever would our future have been if he had succeeded and won the war?

But he didn't!

We are the victors!

For on the 8th of May 'Victory in Europe' is declared. The fighting is almost over!

46

The Ham in the Pram

My baby's lovely new pram is about to be commandeered by her Grandmother to bring sustenance for the family; the war is still on and rationing, which is destined to last for several more years, has parted us from some much missed gastronomic treats.

From the very onset of war, certain foods have disappeared from our lives. Marsh and Baxter advertise in December 1939 that, sadly, there will be no Marsh's hams this Christmas, nor indeed, as it turns out, for a good many Christmases to come.

One of the most noticeable differences for us as a family, having left the hotel behind us, is the lack of food. We are always hungry. Catering coupons gone, we are on the same basic rations as the rest of the population and we don't much like it. Virtually the only culinary high spot in my week now is the entitlement on a Friday to a serving of fish and chips. Oh bliss!

However, my ever-enterprising Mother decides (despite the threat of jail if she is found out) that she will secure a whole ham for us. Some tasty, succulent, home-cured ham. It makes our mouths water. She has heard from a man in the pub that a pig has just been slaughtered.

So she sets off in the early evening armed with the necessary cash.

The problem of how to secrete a large piece of pig between the pub and home is solved by the use of my new baby's pram. Spread with pristine white sheets, it is wheeled up the hill to the pub with excited anticipation. When 10 o'clock strikes and there is still no sign of Mother, I am despatched to find her. I slog up the hill and can see the pram parked at the front of the pub as I approach. People must surely be wondering what sort of irresponsible mother would leave a tiny baby outside a pub till after 10 o'clock at night. I pray quietly to myself that we are not seen by anyone we know who might demand to see my new baby! What a shock that would be!

When I reach the pub, Mother is just preparing to leave. The pram is now loaded with its illicit cargo. Her contact has been late arriving, so she has been obliged to have one or two drinks to pass the time. The steep hill that she negotiated easily uphill with an empty pram earlier in the evening now presents rather more of a challenge in reverse.

The large ham is giving the pram additional weight and impetus; my Mother is quite petite and, with a fair amount of alcohol in her system and a steep downhill gradient, it is not going to be an easy trip home. I am desperate that we do not draw too much attention to ourselves, but we do seem to make an awful lot of noise on the way down .We have made it safely down the hill but goodness knows how. Mother finds it all highly amusing. Father, when we reach home, does not.

So now we are home, Mother in a fit of giggles and Father convinced that we are all about to be jailed. There is a very, very strong smell of ham pervading the street. It does smell very meaty.

Convinced that all our neighbours are already on the way to report our misdemeanour, we push the pram into the safety of the house and hurriedly hang the ham in the cellerette and shut the door, hopeful that we can reduce the smell. This is a vain hope – we can do nothing to diminish the smell; you can detect its delicious but pungent odour throughout the house. It has the capacity to pass through closed doors. We are frightened to open the front door lest the smell links us to the crime. But what are we to do?

It cannot be given away for obvious reasons. The only way forward is to get rid of it as soon as we can. We must eat the evidence as soon as possible! And so the month of eating ham begins, morning, noon and night. By the end we are absolutely sick of it. I never want to see or taste ham ever again. Needless to say, Mother is never tempted to acquire another!

47

The Telegram

On VE-Day and the days and weeks that follow, joyful celebrations are held throughout the country. Street parties are organised, trestle tables laid with colourful cloths, flags of bunting looped from house to house, and Union Jacks draped from windows; everyone is happy. Sandwiches, trifles, jelly and cake; hoarded food is released from special hiding places the rations are being stretched to provide a feast for one and all. Fireworks and bonfires are lit; any symbol of freedom from the tyranny that we had been dreading.

Sadly though, at John's parents' home, the family are in no mood for a celebration. Although they know that John is safe (he is still in the desert making sand yachts in his leisure time, in an attempt to satisfy his need for speed), cousin Derek is OK and daughter Megan is at home, but no one has heard from Rex for months. All they know is that he has been fighting along with his unit at the very heart of the battle somewhere in Europe, and that his whereabouts are unknown. Their brave, young, heroic son is missing.

And then a truly heart-stopping moment occurs. The letterbox rattles, the doorbell rings and there is a delivery boy at the door with a telegram in his hand. It is addressed to W.B. Fellows, the head of the household, Rex's father. This is the one communication dreaded by all in times of war because it is almost always the harbinger of dreadful news. This missive usually carries the few terse lines announcing, 'It is with deep regret that we have to inform you that your loved one (son, daughter, brother, sister or husband) is missing or dead.'

The telegram is carried with due reverence into the dining room, and placed on the bureau where everyone stares at it as if it could suddenly reveal its contents without being opened. Not one of them is brave enough to open it and reveal its contents. They all feel sure that through some rotten irony this gallant young officer had not made it. Victory in Europe suddenly takes on a sour note. What good is victory if the war has taken your youngest child or your kid brother? Eventually, Megan decides that she can stand it no longer and must take matters into her own hands and relieve the agony that they are all suffering.

She opens the envelope and reads aloud the message:

The war is over. Stop.
I am well. Stop.
On my way home. Stop.
Rex.

The very next day the sound of boots coming up the entry announce the return of the hero. Rex is home, safe and sound.

His parents and family are overjoyed, but the worry throughout the war years regarding the wellbeing of her two soldier sons takes a terrible toll on their mother, whose health never quite recovers from the stress of it all.

48

The War is Over!

Although the fighting is over in Europe, the war still continues in the East. Since the bombing of Pearl Harbour in 1941, when the Japanese had decimated the American fleet, America had joined us in the fight (some said better late than never, and so it proves to be). For it is American nuclear bombs that bring the final awful episode of this war finally to a halt. It necessitates the dropping of not one but two atomic bombs in August before the Japanese finally surrender. When the first bomb does not bring them to their knees, a second one is dropped. The devastation is unbelievable but they finally give in when the Emperor, inspecting the damage and seeing the annihilation of the two cities, finally concedes defeat.

On the 15th of August 'Victory in Japan' is declared. It truly is all over.

Three days later, on the 18th of August, it is my twenty-first birthday.

The defeat of the Japanese frees Gloria's cousin Geoff from his three-and-a-half year ordeal in captivity The taking of so many Japanese lives in such a meteoric manner saves his life and that of the other prisoners. Very much longer and he would not have survived; many of those captured with him have not made it. His health has been broken by the ill treatment, but he is alive. Stick thin and hollow-eyed, it takes over two months for him to get home, including a frustrating time held in quarantine in America, but he arrives back in time to attend her wedding. It takes years of treatment to return him to anything like normal health.

We are lucky that we have all survived, when so many did not, but all ours lives have been changed forever by this war.

Being at peace seems odd after so long at war; we have almost become used to the misery. Now everything is going to be different.

The euphoria of Victory passes; peace presents many problems. Houses are hard to find, jobs thin on the ground.

Many of the returning troops find unemployment as a prize for their valiant efforts. Rationing is to continue for some years. For the winners of the war come deprivations and shortages. Many men and women who feel that they had found their true role in the services are now rudderless, disappointed and drifting. Some, having developed relationships with fellow service personnel on overseas postings, have to come round to the realisation that these relationships are doomed and have no possible future. They return to partners and families that they barely know. Wives have to come to terms with the homecoming of complete strangers. The sights and experiences of the conflict have changed the man they love forever; having to cope and make decisions alone has changed their wives. Children do not recognise their fathers and they in turn resent this intruder who is taking Mummy's attention away. Many families must live with the consequences of rushed marriages, of unions struck on the white-hot forge of warfare. Many who have married in haste are forced to repent at leisure.

There is a huge amount of adjusting to do.

But thank God, at last, this dreadful war is over.